Classic Readings in Cultural Anthropology

GARY FERRARO
The University of North Carolina at Charlotte

Australia • Canada • Mexico • Singapore • Spain
United Kingdom • United States

Executive Editor: *Eve Howard*
Acquisitions Editor: *Lin Marshall*
Assistant Editor: *Analie Barnett*
Editorial Assistant: *Amanda Santana*
Technology Project Manager: *Dee Dee Zobian*
Marketing Manager: *Diane Wenckebach*
Marketing Assistant: *Michael Silverstein*
Advertising Project Manager: *Linda Yip*
Project Manager, Editorial Production: *Ritchie Durdin*
Print/Media Buyer: *Rebecca Cross*
Permissions Editor: *Sarah Harkrader*
Production Service: *Shepherd, Inc.*
Copy Editor: *Michele Livingston*
Cover Designer: *Stephen Rapley*
Cover Image: *©2002 Peter Menzel*
Cover Printer: *Webcom*
Compositor: *Shepherd, Inc.*
Printer: *Webcom*

Printed in Canada
1 2 3 4 5 6 7 07 06 05 04 03

For more information about our products, contact us at:
Thomson Learning Academic Resource Center
1-800-423-0563
For permission to use material from this text, contact us by: **Phone:** 1-800-730-2214
Fax: 1-800-730-2215
Web: http://www.thomsonrights.com

Library of Congress Control Number: 2003102730

ISBN: 0–534–61272–5

Wadsworth/Thomson Learning
10 Davis Drive
Belmont, CA 94002-3098
USA

Asia
Thomson Learning
5 Shenton Way #01-01
UIC Building
Singapore 068808

Australia/New Zealand
Thomson Learning
102 Dodds Street
Southbank, Victoria 3006
Australia

Canada
Nelson
1120 Birchmount Road
Toronto, Ontario M1K 5G4
Canada

Europe/Middle East/Africa
Thomson Learning
High Holborn House
50/51 Bedford Row
London WC1R 4LR
United Kingdom

Latin America
Thomson Learning
Seneca, 53
Colonia Polanco
11560 Mexico D.F.
Mexico

Spain/Portugal
Paraninfo
Calle/Magallanes, 25
28015 Madrid, Spain

To all of the authors of classic readings who have been my teachers.

Contents

Preface

It has been estimated that there are over five thousand different cultures in the world today which speak mutually unintelligible languages. With such enormous linguistic and cultural variability in the world, it is virtually impossible to become conversant with *all* of the details of *all* of these different cultures. Thus, by necessity, the study of cultural anthropology at the introductory level needs to take a more conceptual approach. Beginning students, in other words, are exposed typically to certain core ideas, which provide a conceptual framework for studying comparative cultures. Introductory textbooks, for example, are organized around such chapters as marriage and family, which, in turn, cover such key concepts as polygyny, the levirate, arranged marriages, the sororate, cross-cousin marriage, and bridewealth. These central concepts are defined and illustrated with ethnographic data from around the world.

Admittedly introductory textbooks in cultural anthropology take a broad brush approach to a vast subject matter. The emphasis, by necessity, is to expose beginning students to the enormity of cultural variability, while at the same time allowing them to see universal similarities among the cultures of the world. This general approach to studying other cultures, however, can be enhanced by supplemental readings, which permit the student to explore some areas of the subject matter in greater depth. It is with this idea of "post holing" in mind that *Classic Readings in Cultural Anthropology* was conceived.

This reader was carefully designed so as to include those articles and segments from books that best represent the discipline over the course of the past century. These readings were not selected because they represent the most recent research and cutting-edge thinking of twenty first-century scholars. Rather, they represent writings which have been assigned to introductory students by their professors for the past sixty plus years. While being eminently relevant for cultural anthropology today, these selections have endured the decades to become classics in the field. As one anthropologist has put it, these readings are the "gold standard" for modern cultural anthropology.

The readings found in *Classic Readings in Cultural Anthropology* were selected after consulting with a number of cultural anthropologists, including some leading authors of introductory textbooks. Included are pieces dating back as early as 1937 (Evans Pritchard's study of witchcraft among the Azande) and as recently as the 1990s (Deborah Tannen's work on gender differences in language). It should be pointed out that selections were not excluded because they contain terminology that is considered politically incorrect today. In some of the earlier writings, for example, we will see such terms as *man* used to refer generically to humans or the use of the term *Eskimo* instead of the more current term *Inuit*. Nevertheless, the use of these outdated terms (which were not politically incorrect at the time they were written) does not invalidate the relevance of these writings for contemporary cultural anthropology.

Classic Readings in Cultural Anthropology is organized according to the major categories found in most introductory courses of cultural anthropology. These include perspectives on culture, language and communication, ecology and economics, marriage and family, politics and social control, supernatural belief systems, and issues of culture change. The timeless "Body Ritual Among the Nacirema" is as relevant today as it was when it was written by Horace Miner nearly a half century ago, for it forces us to confront our own ethnocentrism. George Gmelch reminds us that despite the fact that Americans view themselves as highly rational, scientific, and objective, they often rely on supernatural forces (such as rituals, taboos, and fetishes) to bring about desired outcomes. In the selection on the potlatch practiced by Native Americans on the northwest coast of the United States, Marvin Harris demonstrates the need to interpret a cultural item within its own cultural context, rather than trying to make sense of it from the perspective of one's own culture. And, Lauriston Sharp's piece on the Yir Yoront remains today (five decades after it was written) a vivid example of the principle of the functional interconnectedness of the parts of culture.

The reader contains a number of pedagogical features designed to help the beginning student learn the content of cultural anthropology more efficiently. First, each reading is preceded by a brief introduction, which helps the reader better understand both the article's relevance and context. Second, a series of "Discussion Questions" at the end of each piece serves not only as a check on understanding, but also as a means to stimulate lively class discussions and encourage the reader to make connections to their everyday lives. Third, a "Resources on the Internet" section follows the discussion questions and enables students to access recent information related to each article.

The purpose of this reader is to provide beginning students of cultural anthropology with a set of readings that have stood the test of time. To ensure that this selection of readings meets your needs as both students and instructors, I encourage you to send me your thoughts on how we can improve upon this volume. Please send your comments to me at *gpferrar@email.uncc.edu*

Gary Ferraro
The University of North Carolina at Charlotte

Introduction

In a recent article in the *Anthropology Newsletter,* anthropologists Bird and Von Trapp report on a nonscientific survey they conducted among a hundred undergraduates that had never taken a course in anthropology. Many of the common stereotypes about anthropology were confirmed. The majority of respondents associated the discipline with stones and bones exclusively; very few could cite the name of a real anthropologist other than the fictional Indiana Jones; and the image of the anthropologist that emerged was a person who was drab, eccentric, elderly, bookish, unbusiness-like, disheveled, wears shabby clothes, and has very little to do with anything outside of academia. All of these impressions are misleading stereotypes, which do nothing but obscure the nature of the discipline and its relevance beyond academia.

Of all of the social sciences, anthropology is the most broadly defined. Some anthropologists do, in fact, deal primarily with stones and bones. One branch of anthropology *(archaeology)* searches for artifacts and other cultural remains of people who lived in the distant past. The subfield of *physical anthropology* unearths fossil remains for the purpose of reconstructing the human evolutionary record. Yet, there are other anthropologists (*cultural anthropologists* and *linguists*) whose focus is on live, warm bodies (i.e., living cultures). Even though these different branches of anthropology have different research agendas, they are all directed at a single purpose: the scientific study of humans, both biologically and culturally, wherever and whenever they may be found. This volume deals only with cultural anthropology, defined most simply as the comparative study of contemporary peoples throughout the world.

Even cultural anthropology, when contrasted with other social sciences, tends to be a wide-ranging discipline. Political scientists focus on power relationships among a group of people. Economists confine their studies to how people produce, distribute, and consume goods and services. Sociologists concentrate on social interaction as their major theoretical construct. Cultural anthropologists, on the other hand, do not limit themselves to a single domain of activity. Rather, by focusing on the concept of culture, cultural anthropologists look at *all* aspects of behavior, attitudes, beliefs, and material possessions. This comprehensive perspective on the study of human behavior makes cultural anthropology particularly effective at helping us better understand people different from ourselves.

What do we mean by the term *culture?* Although we all think we know what culture is, anthropologists have a considerably different definition than the one popularly held. In everyday usage, the term *culture* refers to the finer things in life, such refinements as symphonies, great works of art, and fine wines. In other words, the so-called cultured person prefers Bach to Britney Spears, spends time at art openings rather than at the NASCAR track, and drinks expensive French champagne rather than Bud Light. Cultural anthropologists, however, define the term *culture* much more broadly to include the total lifeways of a group of people. This anthropological definition of culture involves much more than playing cello in a string quartet or eating pheasant under glass. For the anthropologist, a culture encompasses all aspects of a group's behavior, attitudes, beliefs, and material possessions—both the artistic and the mundane. Shaking hands, brushing one's teeth, visiting Aunt Maude, or eating a hot dog are all part of the widely defined anthropological definition of the term *culture.*

But what is it that enables the discipline of cultural anthropology to so effectively reveal human nature? To be certain, cultural anthropologists over the past century have adhered to certain guiding principles, which have distinguished them from other social scientists. First, anthropologists take a highly comparative approach by examining cultural similarities and differences throughout the world. Such an approach serves as a valuable corrective against the pitfall of explaining all human behavior in terms of one's own culture. A case in point is the revision of a prominent psychological theory in the early twentieth century in light of comparative, cross-cultural data from Melanesia. Bronislaw Malinowski, one of the founders of modern anthropology, spent four years of uninterrupted fieldwork among the Trobriand Islanders of the Pacific between 1914 and 1918. At the time, a widely held theory of psychotherapy was the Oedipus Complex, in which Sigmund Freud explained the social/psychological tension between fathers and sons as the result of sexual jealousy over the mother. Freud reasoned that, since all males have an innate desire to have sexual relations with their mother, they are jealous of their fathers, who, in fact, do have such sexual relations.

However, Malinowski's research among the matrilineal Trobrianders revealed no social or psychological tension between a man and his biological father, as was common in western Europe where Freud made his observations.

The Trobriand Islanders made the distinction between a man's *biological* father (who actually impregnated the mother) and his *social* father (who is actually the man's maternal uncle). Malinowski found that in Trobriand society there was considerable tension with the social father (the man actually responsible for his upbringing) and little or no tension with the biological father, who was more like an older brother. Clearly everyone understood that it was the biological father who slept with the mother to produce the child. Malinowski concluded that the tension between fathers and sons observed by Freud in Europe was in fact the result of authority rather than sexual jealousy, and as a result, the so-called Oedipus Complex was a culture-bound explanation of human behavior. Here, then, is an example of how the broad, comparative approach of cultural anthropology served as a check against an oversimplified explanation of human behavior based solely on evidence from one's own culture.

A second principle that has guided cultural anthropology over the past hundred years has been firsthand observation and inquiry. Many social scientists rely primarily on secondary data such as census data or survey information collected from respondents with whom the scientists never have any face-to-face contact. Cultural anthropologists, by way of contrast, rely on participant observation to a greater extent than any other single data-gathering technique. As its name implies, participant observation involves living in the culture under study while at the same time making systematic observations about it. By engaging in participant observation, cultural anthropologists share in the everyday activities of the local people while making detailed observations of people working, playing, eating, talking, trading, educating, or any other cultural activity. The methodological advantages of hands-on research should be obvious. Since most people appreciate any attempt from outsiders to at least try to live according to their culture, participant observation will, in most cases, improve both rapport and the quality of the data received. Moreover, firsthand research allows the anthropologist to distinguish between what people actually do and what they say they do. Participant-observers, in other words, have the advantage of observing actual behavior rather than relying on hearsay.

Perhaps the single-most important feature that cultural anthropologists bring to the study of other cultures is the insistence upon viewing a foreign cultural object within its proper *cultural context*. Whenever people encounter a foreign cultural item (such as an idea, a material object, or a behavior pattern), the usual tendency is to make sense of it in terms of their own cultural assumptions. They generally ask themselves the question: how does this foreign idea or thing fit into my culture? Of course, since it is not part of their culture, there is absolutely no reason why it should fit in. There is, in other words, nothing in their own culture that would tend to support that particular cultural item. If you really want to understand why this particular idea or thing is part of that foreign culture, it must be examined in terms of that culture, rather than your own.

Perhaps an example would help. Most middle-class North Americans, men and women alike, see no sense in the practice of polygyny (a man having more than one wife at a time). They see it as nonsensical, or worse yet, downright immoral and illegal. And, viewed from the perspective of their own cultural assumptions, they would be right. There is very little in our culture that would support or reinforce the practice of polygyny. In fact, there are many parts of our culture that would be in direct conflict with polygyny, such as our legal system and the norms of Christian churches. Even our economic system is at odds with polygyny, because, in a cash economy such as our own, it makes no economic sense whatsoever to have large numbers of wives and large numbers of children.

However, if we view polygyny from its original cultural context—let us say from the cultural perspective of an East African mixed farming community—it makes a good deal of sense. In fact, given all of the other parts of *that* culture, polygyny is the most logical form of marriage imaginable. First, there is nothing illegal about having more than one wife at a time in East Africa. Second, their traditional agricultural system encourages men to take more than one wife so as to maximize the size of the family. Unlike in the United States where large families are economically irrational, in East Africa the more family members there are to cultivate crops, the better off the entire group will be. Third, the system of social prestige in East Africa is based on the number of wives and overall family size, not material wealth as is the case in our own society. Even women in traditional African societies, wanting to be part of a high-status household, supported their husbands' efforts to take additional wives. And, finally, the practice of polygyny is supported in many East African societies by the traditional religious practice of ancestor worship. Since men are often elevated to the status of ancestor-god upon death, it is only logical that men would want to have large families so they will have large numbers of people worshiping them after they die. A man with one wife and one child would have only a "congregation" of two people!

Thus, cultural anthropology teaches us that if we view a foreign cultural item through our own cultural lens, it is not likely to make much sense. When polygyny is wrenched from it original cultural context in East Africa, there is no way that it can seem rational. The best way to truly understand an item from another culture is to view it from within its proper cultural content. No one is asking you to practice a foreign cultural norm (such as polygyny). In fact, you are not even required to like it. But, if you want to understand the inherent logic of why people in another culture think and behave the way they do (which is the primary objective of the discipline of cultural anthropology), then it is imperative that you follow the lead of cultural anthropology, which from its beginnings has insisted on analyzing the parts of different cultures within their original contexts.

1

Body Ritual Among the Nacirema

HORACE MINER

Since the early decades of the twentieth century, Western anthropologists have concentrated their research on small-scale, technologically simple societies outside of Europe and North America. In that same tradition, Horace Miner, a former professor of sociology and anthropology at the University of Michigan, wrote a piece for the American Anthropologist, *in 1956 about an exotic people called the* Nacirema, *whose central belief is that their susceptibility to disease and ill health can only be averted by engaging in a wide range of rituals and magical practices. Miner's elegant description of this highly ritualistic culture provides what at first glance would be a classic example of an exotic non-Western culture. But as you get further into this article—which is probably the most widely reproduced article in twentieth-century anthropology—you get the feeling that it sounds a little too familiar.*

Unlike Miner himself, the editor of this reader will not try to obscure the true identity of the Nacirema, who, Miner tells us, "live between the Canadian Cree, the Yaqui and Tarahumare of Mexico, and the Carib and Arawak of the Antilles." The Nacirema, of course, are us—middle-class residents of the United States. The name Nacirema is American spelled backwards.

The significance of this first selection, and no doubt the reasons for its enormous popularity among anthropologists, is that it forces us to confront our own ethnocentrism. That is, we tend to view other, non-Western societies as filled with ritual, while automatically assuming that our own behavior is based totally on rational thought. The reason that first-time American readers fail to recognize themselves as Nacirema is because they have never applied such terms as ritual or superstition to their own, everyday, mundane behavior. Their ethnocentrism, in other words, prevents them from seeing their own culture as anything other than normal and natural. But Miner's article, now nearly a half century old, forces us to confront our biases when trying to understand our own culture in relation to others.

From "Body Ritual Among the Nacirema" by Horace Miner in *American Anthropologist,* 58(3): 503–507, 1956. Reprinted with permission from the American Anthropological Association.

The anthropologist has become so familiar with the diversity of ways in which different peoples behave in similar situations that he is not apt to be surprised by even the most exotic customs. In fact, if all of the logically possible combinations of behavior have not been found somewhere in the world, he is apt to suspect that they must be present in some yet undescribed tribe. This point has, in fact, been expressed with respect to clan organization by Murdock (1949: 71). In this light, the magical beliefs and practices of the Nacirema present such unusual aspects that it seems desirable to describe them as an example of the extremes to which human behavior can go.

Professor Linton first brought the ritual of the Nacirema to the attention of anthropologists twenty years ago (1936: 326), but the culture of this people is still very poorly understood. They are a North American group living in the territory between the Canadian Cree, the Yaqui and Tarahumare of Mexico, and the Carib and Arawak of the Antilles. Little is known of their origin, though tradition states that they came from the east. According to Nacirema mythology, their nation was originated by a culture hero, Notgnishaw, who is otherwise known for two great feats of strength—the throwing of a piece of wampum across the river Pa-To-Mac and the chopping down of a cherry tree in which the Spirit of Truth resided.

Nacirema culture is characterized by a highly developed market economy which has evolved in a rich natural habitat. While much of the people's time is devoted to economic pursuits, a large part of the fruits of these labors and a considerable portion of the day are spent in ritual activity. The focus of this activity is the human body, the appearance and health of which loom as a dominant concern in the ethos of the people. While such a concern is certainly not unusual, its ceremonial aspects and associated philosophy are unique.

The fundamental belief underlying the whole system appears to be that the human body is ugly and that its natural tendency is to debility and disease. Incarcerated in such a body, man's only hope is to avert these characteristics through the use of the powerful influences of ritual and ceremony. Every household has one or more shrines devoted to this purpose. The more powerful individuals in the society have several shrines in their houses and, in fact, the opulence of a house is often referred to in terms of the number of such ritual centers it possesses. Most houses are of wattle and daub construction, but the shrine rooms of the more wealthy are walled with stone. Poorer families imitate the rich by applying pottery plaques to their shrine walls.

While each family has at least one such shrine, the rituals associated with it are not family ceremonies but are private and secret. The rites are normally only discussed with children, and then only during the period when they are being initiated into these mysteries. I was able, however, to establish sufficient rapport with the natives to examine these shrines and to have the rituals described to me.

The focal point of the shrine is a box or chest which is built into the wall. In this chest are kept the many charms and magical potions without which no native believes he could live. These preparations are secured from a variety of specialized practitioners. The most powerful of these are the medicine men, whose assistance must be rewarded with substantial gifts. However, the medicine men do not provide the curative potions for their clients, but decide what the ingredients should be and then write them down in an ancient and secret language. This writing is understood only by the medicine men and by the herbalists who, for another gift, provide the required charm.

The charm is not disposed of after it has served its purpose, but is placed in the charm-box of the household shrine. As these magical materials are specific for certain ills, and the real or imagined maladies of the people are many, the charm-box is usually full to overflowing. The magical packets are so numerous that people forget what their purposes were and fear to use them again. While the natives are very vague on this point, we can only assume that the idea in retaining all the old magical materials is that their presence in the charm-box, before which the body rituals are conducted, will in some way protect the worshipper.

Beneath the charm-box is a small font. Each day every member of the family, in succession, enters the shrine room, bows his head before the charm-box, mingles different sorts of holy water in the font, and proceeds with a brief rite of ablution. The holy waters are secured from the Water Temple of the community, where the priests conduct elaborate ceremonies to make the liquid ritually pure.

In the hierarchy of magical practitioners, and below the medicine men in prestige, are specialists whose designation is best translated "holy-mouth-men." The Nacirema have an almost pathological horror and fascination with the mouth, the condition of which is believed to have a supernatural influence on all social relationships. Were it not for the rituals of the mouth, they believe that their teeth would fall out, their gums bleed, their jaws shrink, their friends desert them, and their lovers reject them. (They also believe that a strong relationship exists between oral and moral characteristics. For example, there is a ritual ablution of the mouth for children which is supposed to improve their moral fiber.)

The daily body ritual performed by everyone includes a mouth-rite. Despite the fact that these people are so punctilious about care of the mouth, this rite involves a practice which strikes the uninitiated stranger as revolting. It was reported to me that the ritual consists of inserting a small bundle of hog hairs into the mouth, along with certain magical powders, and then moving the bundle in a highly formalized series of gestures.

In addition to the private mouth-rite, the people seek out a holy-mouth-man once or twice a year. These practitioners have an impressive set of paraphernalia, consisting of a variety of augers, awls, probes, and prods. The use of these objects in the exorcism of the evils of the mouth involves almost unbelievable ritual torture of the client. The holy-mouth-man opens the client's mouth and, using the above mentioned tools, enlarges any holes which decay may have created in the teeth. Magical materials are put into these holes. If there are no naturally occurring holes in the teeth, large sections of one or more teeth are gouged out so that the supernatural substance can be applied. In the client's view, the purpose of these ministrations is to arrest decay and to draw friends. The extremely sacred and traditional character of the rite is evident in the fact that the natives return to the holy-mouth-men year after year, despite the fact that their teeth continue to decay.

It is to be hoped that, when a thorough study of the Nacirema is made, there will be a careful inquiry into the personality structure of these people. One has but to watch the gleam in the eye of a holy-mouth-man, as he jabs an awl into an exposed nerve, to suspect that a certain amount of sadism is involved. If this can be established, a very interesting pattern emerges, for most of the population shows definite masochistic tendencies. It was to these that Professor Linton referred in discussing a distinctive part of the daily body ritual which is performed only by men. This part of the rite involves scraping and lacerating the surface of the face with a sharp instrument. Special women's rites are performed only four times during each lunar month, but what they lack in frequency is made up in barbarity. As part of this ceremony, women bake their heads in small ovens for about an hour. The theoretically interesting point is that what seems to be a preponderantly masochistic people have developed sadistic specialists.

The medicine men have an imposing temple, or *latipso,* in every community of any size. The more elaborate ceremonies required to treat very sick patients can only be performed at this temple. These ceremonies involve not only the thaumaturge but a permanent group of vestal maidens who move sedately about the temple chambers in distinctive costume and headdress.

The *latipso* ceremonies are so harsh that it is phenomenal that a fair proportion of the really sick natives who enter the temple ever recover. Small children whose indoctrination is still incomplete have been known to resist attempts to take them to the temple because "that is where you go to die." Despite this fact, sick adults are not only willing but eager to undergo the protracted ritual purification, if they can afford to do so. No matter how ill the supplicant or how grave the emergency, the guardians of many temples will not admit a client if he cannot give a rich gift to the custodian. Even after one has gained admission and survived the ceremonies, the guardians will not permit the neophyte to leave until he makes still another gift.

The supplicant entering the temple is first stripped of all his or her clothes. In every-day life the Nacirema avoids exposure of his body and its natural functions. Bathing and excretory acts are performed only in the secrecy of the household shrine, where they are ritualized as part of the body-rites. Psychological shock results from the fact that body secrecy is suddenly lost upon entry into the *latipso.* A man, whose own wife has never seen him in an excretory act, suddenly finds himself naked and assisted by a vestal maiden while he performs his natural functions into a sacred vessel. This sort of ceremonial treatment is necessitated by the fact that the excreta are used by a diviner to ascertain the course and nature of the client's sickness. Female clients, on the other hand, find their naked bodies are subjected to the scrutiny, manipulation and prodding of the medicine men.

Few supplicants in the temple are well enough to do anything but lie on their hard beds. The daily ceremonies, like the rites of the holy-mouth-men, involve discomfort and torture. With ritual precision, the vestals awaken their miserable charges each dawn and roll them about on their beds of pain while performing ablutions, in the formal movements of which the maidens are highly trained. At other times they insert magic wands in the supplicant's mouth or force him to eat substances which are supposed to be healing. From time to time the medicine men come to their clients and jab magically treated needles into their flesh. The fact that these temple ceremonies may not cure, and may even kill the neophyte, in no way decreases the people's faith in the medicine men.

There remains one other kind of practioner, known as a "listener." This witch-doctor has the power to exorcise the devils that lodge in the heads of people who have been bewitched. The Nacirema believe that parents bewitch their own children. Mothers are particularly suspected of putting a curse on children while teaching them the secret body rituals. The counter-magic of the witch-doctor is unusual in its lack of ritual. The patient simply tells the "listener" all his troubles and fears, beginning with the earliest difficulties he can remember. The memory displayed by the Nacirema in these exorcism sessions is truly remarkable. It is not uncommon for the patient to bemoan the rejection he felt upon being weaned as a babe. and a few individuals even see their troubles going back to the traumatic effects of their own birth.

In conclusion, mention must be made of certain practices which have their base in native esthetics but which depend upon the pervasive aversion to the natural body and its functions. There are ritual fasts to make fat people thin and ceremonial feasts to make thin people fat. Still other rites are used to make women's breasts large if they are small, and smaller if they are large. General dissatisfaction with breast shape is symbolized in the fact that the ideal form is virtually outside the range of human variation. A few women afflicted with almost inhuman hyper-mammary development are so idolized that they make a handsome living by simply going from village to village and permitting the natives to stare at them for a fee.

Reference has already been made to the fact that excretory functions are ritualized, routinized, and relegated to secrecy. Natural reproductive functions are similarly distorted. Intercourse is taboo as a topic and scheduled as an act. Efforts are made to avoid pregnancy by the use of magical materials or by limiting intercourse to certain phases of the moon. Conception is actually very infrequent. When pregnant, women dress so as to hide their condition. Parturition takes place in secret, without friends or relatives to assist, and the majority of women do not nurse their infants.

Our review of the ritual life of the Nacirema has certainly shown them to be a magic-ridden people. It is hard to understand how they have managed to exist so long under the burdens which they have imposed upon themselves. But even such exotic customs as these take on real meaning when they are viewed with the insight provided by Malinowski when he wrote (1948: 70):

> Looking from far and above, from our high places of safety in the developed civilization, it is easy to see all the crudity and irrelevance of magic. But without its power and guidance early man could not have mastered his practical difficulties as he has done, nor could man have advanced to the higher stages of civilization.

REFERENCES

Linton, Ralph. 1936. *The Study of Man.* New York: D. Appleton-Century Co.

Malinowski, Bronislaw. 1948. *Magic, Science, and Religion.* Glencoe: The Free Press.

Murdock, George P. 1949. *Social Structure.* New York: The Macmillan Co.

DISCUSSION QUESTIONS

1. What does Miner's piece tell us about the difficulty of describing another culture?
2. What other areas of U.S. culture could you write about in a fashion similar to this reading? It might be interesting to write an "outsider" description of the "American VUS."
3. How effective are the potions and magical cures found in the Nacirema charm boxes? Is this an important question for cultural anthropologists to answer?

RESOURCES ON THE INTERNET

InfoTrac College Edition

(http://infotrac.thomsonlearning.com/index.html)

You can find further relevant readings by searching *InfoTrac College Edition,* an online library with access to thousands of scholarly and popular periodicals. Below are suggested search terms for this article:

- ritual
- ceremony
- superstition

Anthropology Online: Wadsworth's Anthropology Resource Center

(http://anthropology.wadsworth.com)

The Wadsworth Anthropology Resource Center contains a wealth of information and useful tools for students including information on careers in anthropology.

2

Queer Customs

CLYDE KLUCKHOHN

In this selection, written more than half a century ago, Clyde Kluckhohn explains the anthropological concept of culture in a way that is eminently understandable for the beginning student of comparative cultures. Referring to culture as a "design for living," Kluckhohn, who for much of his career was the leading authority on the Navajo, used the anthropological perspective to explain what most nonanthropologists at the time considered to be "queer customs." He examined culture by showing how it is different from biological influences on our behavior, how culture influences biological processes, how it is learned rather than being genetically transmitted, and how it functions to help people adapt to their environment. Even though some of his references are today politically incorrect (for example, the use of such terms as primitive and heathen), Kluckhohn's piece serves as a valuable reminder that the study of other cultures allows us to better understand our own culture.

Why do the Chinese dislike milk and milk products? Why would the Japanese die willingly in a Banzai charge that seemed senseless to Americans? Why do some nations trace descent through the father, others through the mother, still others through both parents? Not because different peoples have different instincts, not because they were destined by God or Fate to different habits, not because the weather is different in China and Japan and the United States. Sometimes shrewd common sense has an answer that is close to that of the anthropologist: "because they were brought up that way." By "culture" anthropology means the total life way of a people, the social legacy the individual acquires from his group. Or culture can be regarded as that part of the environment that is the creation of man.

This technical term has a wider meaning than the "culture" of history and literature. A humble cooking pot is as much a cultural product as is a Beethoven sonata. In ordinary speech a man of culture is a man who can speak languages other than his own, who is familiar with history, literature, philosophy, or the fine arts. In some cliques that definition is still narrower. The cultured person is one who can talk about James Joyce, Scarlatti, and Picasso. To the anthropologist, however, to be human is to be cultured. There is culture in general, and then there are the specific cultures such as Russian, American, British, Hottentot, Inca. The general abstract notion services to remind us that we cannot explain acts solely in terms of the biological properties of the people concerned, their individual past experience, and the immediate situation. The past experience of other men in the form of culture enters into almost every event. Each specific culture constitutes a kind of blueprint for all of life's activities.

From *Mirror for Man: Anthropology and Modern Life* by Clyde Kluckhohn, pp. 17–27. Used with permission.

One of the interesting things about human beings is that they try to understand themselves and their own behavior. While this has been particularly true of Europeans in recent times, there is no group which has not developed a scheme or schemes to explain man's actions. To the insistent human query "why?" the most exciting illumination anthropology has to offer is that of the concept of culture. Its explanatory importance is comparable to categories such as evolution in biology, gravity in physics, disease in medicine. A good deal of human behavior can be understood, and indeed predicted, if we know a people's design for living. Many acts are neither accidental nor due to personal pecularities nor caused by supernatural forces nor simply mysterious. Even those of us who pride ourselves on our individualism follow most of the time a pattern not of our own making. We brush our teeth on arising. We put on pants—not a loincloth or a grass skirt. We eat three meals a day—not four or five or two. We sleep in a bed—not in a hammock or on a sheep pelt. I do not have to know the individual and his life history to be able to predict these and countless other regularities, including many in the thinking process, of all Americans who are not incarcerated in jails or hospitals for the insane.

To the American woman a system of plural wives seems "instinctively" abhorrent. She cannot understand how any woman can fail to be jealous and uncomfortable if she must share her husband with other women. She feels it "unnatural" to accept such a situation. On the other hand, a Koryak woman of Siberia, for example, would find it hard to understand how a woman could be so selfish and so undesirous of femine companionship in the home as to wish to restrict her husband to one mate.

Some years ago I met in New York City a young man who did not speak a word of English and was obviously bewildered by American ways. By "blood" he was as American as you or I, for his parents had gone from Indiana to China as missionaries. Orphaned in infancy, he was reared by a Chinese family in a remote village. All who met him found him more Chinese than American. The facts of his blue eyes and light hair were less impressive than a Chinese style of gait, Chinese arm and hand movements, Chinese facial expression, and Chinese modes of thought. The biological heritage was American, but the cultural training had been Chinese. He returned to China.

Another example of another kind: I once knew a trader's wife in Arizona who took a somewhat devilish interest in producing a cultural reaction. Guests who came her way were often served delicious sandwiches filled with a meat that seemed to be neither chicken nor tuna fish yet was reminiscent of both. To queries she gave no reply until each had eaten his fill. She then explained that what they had eaten was not chicken, not tuna fish, but the rich, white flesh of freshly killed rattlesnakes. The response was instantaneous—vomiting, often violent vomiting. A biological process is caught in a cultural web.

A highly intelligent teacher with long and successful experience in the public schools of Chicago was finishing her first year in an Indian school. When asked how her Navaho pupils compared in intelligence with Chicago youngsters, she replied, "Well, I just don't know. Sometimes the Indians seem just as bright. At other times they just act like dumb animals. The other night we had a dance in the high school. I saw a boy who is one of the best students in my English class standing off by himself. So I took him over to a pretty girl and told them to dance. But they just stood there with their heads down. They wouldn't even say anything." I inquired if she knew whether or not they were members of the same clan. "What difference would that make?"

"How would you feel about getting into bed with your brother?" The teacher walked off in a huff, but, actually, the two cases were quite comparable in principle. To the Indian the type of bodily contact involved in our social dancing has a directly sexual connotation. The incest taboos between members of the same clan are as severe as between true brothers and sisters. The shame of the Indians at the suggestion that a clan brother and sister should dance and the indignation of the white teacher at the idea that she should share a bed with an adult brother represent equally nonrational responses, culturally standardized unreason.

All this does not mean that there is no such thing as raw human nature. The very fact that certain of the same institutions are found in all known societies indicates that at bottom all human beings are very much alike. The files of the Cross-Cultural Survey at Yale University are organized according to categories such as "marriage ceremonies," "life crisis rites," "incest taboos." At least seventy-five of these categories are represented in every single one of the hundreds of cultures analyzed. This is hardly surprising. The members of all human groups have about the same biological equipment. All men undergo the same poignant life experiences such as birth, helplessness, illness, old age, and death. The biological potentialities of the species are the blocks with which cultures are built. Some patterns of every culture crystallize around focuses provided by the inevitables of biology: the difference between the sexes, the presence of persons of different ages, the varying physical strength and skill of individuals. The facts of nature also limit culture forms. No culture provides patterns for jumping over trees or for eating iron ore.

There is thus no "either-or" between nature and that special form of nurture called culture. Culture determinism is as one-sided as biological determinism. The two factors are interdependent. Culture arises out of human nature, and its forms are restricted both by man's biology and by natural laws. It is equally true that culture channels biological processes—vomiting, weeping, fainting, sneezing, the daily habits of food intake and waste elimination. When a man eats, he is reacting to an internal "drive," namely, hunger contractions consequent upon the lowering of blood sugar, but his precise reaction to these internal stimuli cannot be predicted by physiological knowledge alone. Whether a healthy adult feels hungry twice, three times, or four times a day and the hours at which this feeling recurs is a question of culture. *What* he eats is of course limited by availability, but is also partly regulated by culture. It is a biological fact that some types of berries are poisonous; it is a cultural fact that, a few generations ago, most Americans considered tomatoes to be poisonous and refused to eat them. Such selective, discriminative use of the environment is characteristically cultural. In a still more general sense, too, the process of eating is channeled by culture. Whether a man eats to live, lives to eat, or merely eats and lives is only in part an individual matter, for there are also cultural trends. Emotions are physiological events. Certain situations will evoke fear in people from any culture. But sensations of pleasure, anger, and lust may be stimulated by cultural cues that would leave unmoved someone who has been reared in a different social tradition.

Except in the case of newborn babies and of individuals born with clear-cut structural or functional abnormalities we can observe innate endowments only as modified by cultural training. In a hospital in New Mexico where Zuñi Indian, Navaho Indian, and white American babies are born, it is possible to classify the newly arrived infants as unusually active, average, and quiet. Some babies from each "racial" group will fall into each category, though a higher proportion of the white babies will fall into the unusually active class. But if a Navaho baby, a Zuñi baby, and a white baby—all classified as unusually active at birth—are again observed at the age of two years, the Zuñi baby will no longer seem given to quick and restless activity—*as compared with the white child*—though he may seem so as compared with the other Zuñis of the same age. The Navaho child is likely to fall in between as contrasted with the Zuñi and the white, though he will probably still seem more active than the average Navaho youngster.

It was remarked by many observers in the Japanese relocation centers that Japanese who were born and brought up in this country, especially those who were reared apart from any large colony of Japanese, resemble in behavior their white neighbors much more closely than they do their own parents who were educated in Japan.

I have said "culture channels biological processes." It is more accurate to say "the biological functioning of individuals is modified if they have been trained in certain ways and not in others." Culture is not a disembodied force. It is created and transmitted by people. However, culture, like well-known concepts of the physical sciences, is a convenient abstraction. One never sees gravity. One sees bodies falling in regular ways. One never sees an electromagnetic field. Yet certain happenings that can be seen may be given a neat abstract formulation by assuming that the electromagnetic field exists. Similarly, one never sees culture as such. What is seen are regularities in the behavior or artifacts of a group that has adhered to a common tradition. The regularities in style and technique of ancient Inca tapestries or stone axes from Melanesian islands are due to the existence of mental blueprints for the group.

Culture is a *way* of thinking, feeling, believing. It is the group's knowledge stored up (in memories of men; in books and objects) for future use. We study the products of this "mental" activity: the overt behavior, the speech and gestures and activities of people, and the tangible results of these things such as tools, houses, cornfields, and what not. It has been customary in lists of "culture traits" to include such things as watches or lawbooks. This is a convenient way of thinking about them, but in the solution of any important problem we must remember that they, in themselves, are nothing but metals, paper, and ink. What is important is that some men know how to make them, others set a value on them, are unhappy without them, direct their activities in relation to them, or disregard them.

It is only a helpful shorthand when we say "The cultural patterns of the Zulu were resistant to Christianization." In the directly observable world of course, it was individual Zulus who resisted. Nevertheless, if we do not forget that we are speaking at a high level of abstraction, it is justifiable to speak of culture as a cause. One may compare the practice of saying "syphilis caused the extinction of the native population of the island." Was it "syphilis" or "syphilis germs" or "human beings who were carriers of syphilis?"

"Culture," then, is "a theory." But if a theory is not contradicted by any relevant fact and if it helps us to understand a mass of otherwise chaotic facts, it is useful. Darwin's contribution was much less the accumulation of new knowledge than the creation of a theory which put in order data already known. An accumulation of facts, however large, is no more a science than a pile of bricks is a house. Anthropology's demonstration that the most weird set of customs has a consistency and an order is comparable to modern psychiatry's showing that there is meaning and purpose in the apparently incoherent talk of the insane. In fact, the inability of the older psychologies and philosophies to account for the strange behavior of madmen and heathens was the principal factor that forced psychiatry and anthropology to develop theories of the unconscious and of culture.

Since culture is an abstraction, it is important not to confuse culture with society. A "society" refers to a group of people who interact more with each other than they do with other individuals—who cooperate with each other for the attainment of certain ends. You can see and indeed count the individuals who make up a society. A "culture" refers to the distinctive ways of life of such a group of people. Not all social events are culturally patterned. New types of circumstances arise for which no cultural solutions have as yet been devised.

A culture constitutes a storehouse of the pooled learning of the group. A rabbit starts life with some innate responses. He can learn from his own experience and perhaps from observing other rabbits. A human infant is born with fewer instincts and greater plasticity. His main task is to learn the answers that persons he will never see, persons long dead, have worked out. Once he has learned the formulas supplied by the culture of his group, most of his behavior becomes almost as automatic and unthinking as if it were instinctive. There is a tremendous amount of intelligence behind the making of a radio, but not much is required to learn to turn it on.

The members of all human societies face some of the same unavoidable dilemmas, posed by biology and other facts of the human situation. This is why the basic categories of all cultures are so similar. Human culture without language is unthinkable. No culture fails to provide for aesthetic expression and aesthetic delight. Every culture supplies standardized orientations toward the deeper problems, such as death. Every culture is designed to perpetuate the group and its solidarity, to meet the demands of individuals for an orderly way of life and for satisfaction of biological needs.

However, the variations on these basic themes are numberless. Some languages are built up out of twenty basic sounds, others out of forty. Nose plugs were considered beautiful by the predynastic Egyptians but are not by the modern French. Puberty is a biological fact. But one culture ignores it, another prescribes informal instructions about sex but no ceremony, a third has impressive rites for girls only, a fourth for boys and girls. In this culture, the first menstruation is welcomed as a happy, natural event; in that culture the atmosphere is full of dread and supernatural threat. Each culture dissects nature according to its own system of categories. The Navaho Indians apply the same word to the color of a robin's egg and to that of grass. A psychologist once assumed that this meant a difference in the sense organs, that Navahos didn't have the physiological equipment to distinguish "green" from "blue." However, when he showed them objects of the two colors and asked them if they were exactly the same colors, they looked at him with astonishment. His dream of discovering a new type of color blindness was shattered.

Every culture must deal with the sexual instinct. Some, however, seek to deny all sexual expression before marriage, whereas a Polynesian adolescent who was not promiscuous would be distinctly abnormal. Some cultures enforce lifelong monogamy, others, like our own, tolerate serial monogamy; in still other cultures, two or more women may be joined to one man or several men to a single woman. Homosexuality has been a permitted pattern in the Greco-Roman world, in parts of Islam, and in various primitive tribes. Large portions of the population of Tibet, and of Christendom at some places and periods, have practiced completely celibacy. To us marriage is first and foremost an arrangement between two individuals. In many more societies marriage is merely one facet of a complicated set of reciprocities, economic and otherwise, between two families or two clans.

The essence of the cultural process is selectivity. The selection is only exceptionally conscious and rational. Cultures are like Topsy. They just grew. Once, however, a way of handling a situation becomes institutionalized, there is ordinarily great resistance to change or deviation. When we speak of "our sacred beliefs," we mean of course that they are beyond criticism and that the person who suggests modification or abandonment must be punished. No person is emotionally indifferent to his culture. Certain cultural premises may become totally out of accord with a new factual situation. Leaders may recognize this and reject the old ways in theory. Yet their emotional loyalty continues in the face of reason because of the intimate conditionings of early childhood.

A culture is learned by individuals as the result of belonging to some particular group, and it constitutes that part of learned behavior which is shared with others. It is our social legacy, as contrasted with our organic heredity. It is one of the important factors which permits us to live together in an organized society, giving us ready-made solutions to our problems, helping us to predict the behavior of others, and permitting others to know what to expect of us.

Culture regulates our lives at every turn. From the moment we are born until we die there is, whether we are conscious of it or not, constant pressure upon us to follow certain types of behavior that other men have created for us. Some paths we follow willingly, others we follow because we know no other way, still others we deviate from or go back to most unwillingly. Mothers of small children know how unnaturally most of this comes to us—how little regard we have, until we are "culturalized," for the "proper" place, time, and manner for certain acts such as eating, excreting, sleeping, getting dirty, and making loud noises. But by more or less adhering to a system of related designs for carrying out all the acts of living, a group of men and women feel themselves linked together by a powerful chain of sentiments. Ruth Benedict gave an almost complete definition of the concept when she said, "Culture is that which binds men together."

It is true any culture is a set of techniques for adjusting both to the external environment and to other men. However, cultures create problems as well as solve them. If the lore of a people states that frogs are dangerous creatures, or that it is not safe to go about at night because of witches or ghosts, threats are posed which do not arise out of the inexorable facts of the external world. Cultures produce needs as well as provide a means of fulfilling them. There exists for every group culturally defined, acquired drives that may be more powerful in ordinary daily life than the biologically inborn drives. Many Americans, for example, will work harder for "success" than they will for sexual satisfaction.

Most groups elaborate certain aspects of their culture far beyond maximum utility or survival value. In other words, not all culture promotes physical survival. At times, indeed, it does exactly the opposite. Aspects of culture which once were adaptive may persist long after they have ceased to be useful. An analysis of any culture will disclose many features which cannot possibly be construed as adaptations to the total environment in which the group now finds itself. However, it is altogether likely that these apparently useless features represent survivals, with modifications through time, of cultural forms which were adaptive in one or another previous situation.

Any cultural practice must be functional or it will disappear before long. That is, it must somehow contribute to the survival of the society or to the adjustment of the individual. However, many cultural functions are not manifest but latent. A cowboy will walk three miles to catch a horse which he then rides one mile to the store. From the point of view of manifest function this is positively irrational. But the act has the latent function of maintaining the cowboy's prestige in the terms of his own subculture. One can instance the buttons on the sleeve of a man's coat, our absurd English spelling, the use of capital letters, and a host of other apparently nonfunctional customs. They serve mainly the latent function of assisting individuals to maintain their security by preserving continuity with the past and by making certain sectors of life familiar and predictable.

Every culture is a precipitate of history. In more than one sense history is a sieve. Each culture embraces those aspects of the past which, usually in altered form and with altered meanings, live on in the present. Discoveries and inventions, both material and ideological, are constantly being made available to a group through its historical contacts with other peoples or being created by its own members. However, only those that fit the total immediate situation in meeting the group's needs for survival or in promoting the psychological adjustment of individuals will become part of the culture. The process of culture building may be regarded as an addition to man's innate biological capacities, an addition providing instruments which enlarge, or may even substitute for, biological functions, and to a degree compensating for biological limitations—as in ensuring that death does not always result in the loss to humanity of what the deceased has learned.

Culture is like a map. Just as a map isn't the territory but an abstract representation of a particular area, so also a culture is an abstract description of trends toward uniformity in the words, deeds, and artifacts of a human group. If a map is accurate and you can read it, you won't get lost; if you know a culture, you will know your way around in the life of a society. Many educated people have the notion that culture applies only to exotic ways of life or to societies where relative simplicity and relative homogeneity prevail. Some sophisticated missionaries, for example, will use the anthropological conception in discussing the special modes of living of South Sea Islanders, but seem amazed at the idea that it could be applied equally to inhabitants of New York City. And social workers in Boston will talk about the culture of a colorful and well-knit immigrant group but boggle at applying it to the behavior of staff members in the social-service agency itself.

In the primitive society the correspondence between the habits of individuals and the customs of the community is ordinarily greater. There is probably some truth in what an old Indian once said, "In the old days there was no law; everybody did what was right." The primitive tends to find happiness in the fulfillment of intricately involuted cultural patterns; the modern more often tends to feel the pattern as repressive to his individuality. It is also true that in a complex stratified society there are numerous exceptions to generalizations made about the culture as a whole. It is necessary to study regional, class, and occupational subcultures. Primitive cultures have greater stability than modern cultures; they change—but less rapidly.

However, modern men also are creators and carriers of culture. Only in some respects are they influenced differently from primitives by culture. Moreover, there are such wide variations in primitive cultures that any black-and-white contrast between the primitive and the civilized is altogether fictitious. The distinction which is most generally true lies in the field of conscious philosophy.

The publication of Paul Radin's *Primitive Man as a Philosopher* did much toward destroying the myth that an abstract analysis of experience was a peculiarity of literate societies.

DISCUSSION QUESTIONS

1. What does Kluckhohn mean when he says that "culture channels biological processes"? Can you think of any contemporary examples of this principle?
2. What is meant by the nature-nurture debate?
3. The title of the book from which this selection is taken is *Mirror for Man.* What is the meaning of this title?

RESOURCES ON THE INTERNET

InfoTrac College Edition

(http://infotrac.thomsonlearning.com/index.html)

You can find further relevant readings by searching *InfoTrac College Edition,* an online library with access to thousands of scholarly and popular periodicals. Below are suggested search terms for this article:

- custom
- trait
- environment

Anthropology Online: Wadsworth's Anthropology Resource Center

(http://anthropology.wadsworth.com)

The Wadsworth Anthropology Resource Center contains a wealth of information and useful tools for students including information on careers in anthropology.

3

Rapport-talk and Report-talk

DEBORAH TANNEN

In the selection, Deborah Tannen, a professor of sociolinguistics at Georgetown University, explores the very real differences in linguistic style between men and women in the United States. Women feel that men never express their feelings, are critical, and tend to operate in "lecture mode." Men, on the other hand, feel that their wives nag them and never get to the point. Often women and men walk away from a conversation with totally different impressions of what has just transpired. In many respects, Tannen suggests that discourse between men and women takes on some of the difficulties of cross-cultural communication.

Tannen distinguishes between the female mode of "rapport-talk" and the male mode of "report-talk." Women, according to Tannen, use talk for the purpose of building rapport with others. This rapport-talk involves a good deal of emotional self-disclosure and emphasizes matching experiences and showing empathy and understanding. Report-talk, on the other hand, the prominent linguistic style of men, uses talk to establish and maintain status and power. Personal disclosures are avoided because they can make the highly combative male appear vulnerable. For men discourse is competitive, information-oriented, and geared to solving problems and accomplishing goals. Men feel more comfortable engaging in public speaking while women operate more effectively in the private domain.

It is no coincidence that the book from which this selection is taken stayed on the New York Times *best-seller list for nearly four years. Tannen combines a keen eye for observation with the power of original analysis to provide an excellent description of gender discourse in the United States. But Tannen's work is also relevant to applied anthropology because of its usefulness for helping us better understand and improve our discourse with members of the opposite sex.*

I was sitting in a suburban living room, speaking to a women's group that had invited men to join them for the occasion of my talk about communication between women and men. During the discussion, one man was particularly talkative, full of lengthy comments and explanations. When I made the observation that women often complain that their husbands don't talk to them enough, this man volunteered that he heartily agreed. He gestured toward his wife, who had sat silently beside him on the couch throughout the evening, and said, "She's the talker in our family."

Everyone in the room burst into laughter. The man looked puzzled and hurt. "It's true," he explained. "When I come home from work, I usually have nothing to say, but she never runs out. If it weren't for her, we'd spend the whole evening in silence." Another woman expressed a similar paradox about her husband: "When we go out, he's the life of the party. If I happen to be in another room, I can always hear his voice above the others. But when we're home, he doesn't have that much to say. I do most of the talking."

Who talks more, women or men? According to the stereotype, women talk too much. Linguist Jennifer Coates notes some proverbs:

> A woman's tongue wags like a lamb's tail.
>
> Foxes are all tail and women are all tongue.
>
> The North Sea will sooner be found wanting in water than a woman be at a loss for a word.

Throughout history, women have been punished for talking too much or in the wrong way. Linguist Connie Eble lists a variety of physical punishments used in Colonial America: Women were strapped to dunking stools and held underwater until they nearly drowned, put into the stocks with signs pinned to them, gagged, and silenced by a cleft stick applied to their tongues.

Though such institutionalized corporal punishments have given way to informal, often psychological ones, modern stereotypes are not much different from those expressed in the old proverbs. Women are believed to talk too much. Yet study after study finds that it is men who talk more—at meetings, in mixed-group discussions, and in classrooms where girls or young women sit next to boys or young men. For example, communications researchers Barbara and Gene Eakins tape-recorded and studied seven university faculty meetings. They found that, with one exception, men spoke more often and, without exception, spoke for a longer time. The men's turns ranged from 10.66 to 17.07 seconds, while the women's turns ranged from 3 to 10 seconds. In other words, the women's longest turns were still shorter than the men's shortest turns.

When a public lecture is followed by questions from the floor, or a talk show host opens the phones, the first voice to be heard asking a question is almost always a man's. And when they ask questions or offer comments from the audience, men tend to talk longer. Linguist Marjorie Swacker recorded question-and-answer sessions at academic conferences. Women were highly visible as speakers at the conferences studied; they presented 40.7 percent of the papers at the conferences studied and made up 42 percent of the audiences. But when it came to volunteering and being called on to ask questions, women contributed only 27.4 percent. Furthermore, the women's questions, on the average, took less than half as much time as the men's. (The mean was 23.1 seconds for women, 52.7 for men.) This happened, Swacker shows, because men (but not women) tended to preface their questions with statements, ask more than one question, and follow up the speaker's answer with another question or comment.

I have observed this pattern at my own lectures, which concern issues of direct relevance to women. Regardless of the proportion of women and men in the audience, men almost invariably ask the first question, more questions, and longer questions. In these situations, women often feel that men are talking too much. I recall one discussion period following a lecture I gave to a group assembled in a bookstore. The group was composed mostly of women, but most of the discussion was being conducted by men in the audience. At one point, a man sitting in the middle was talking at such great length that several women in the front rows began shifting in their seats and rolling their eyes at me. Ironically, what he was going on about was how frustrated he feels when he has to listen to women going on and on about topics he finds boring and unimportant.

RAPPORT-TALK AND REPORT-TALK

Who talks more, then, women or men? The seemingly contradictory evidence is reconciled by the difference between what I call *public* and *private speaking*. More men feel comfortable doing "public speaking," while more women feel comfortable doing "private" speaking. Another way of capturing these differences is by using the terms *report-talk* and *rapport-talk*.

For most women, the language of conversation is primarily a language of rapport: a way of establishing connections and negotiating relationships. Emphasis is placed on displaying similarities and matching experiences. From childhood, girls criticize peers who try to stand out or appear better than others. People feel their closest connections at home, or in settings where they *feel* at home—with one or a few people they feel close to and comfortable with—in other words, during private speaking. But even the most public situations can be approached like private speaking.

For most men, talk is primarily a means to preserve independence and negotiate and maintain status in a hierarchical social order. This is done by exhibiting knowledge and skill, and by holding center stage through verbal performance such as storytelling, joking, or imparting information. From childhood, men learn to use talking as a way to get and keep attention. So they are more comfortable speaking in larger groups made up of people they know less well—in the broadest sense, "public speaking." But even the most private situations can be approached like public speaking, more like giving a report than establishing rapport.

PRIVATE SPEAKING: THE WORDY WOMAN AND THE MUTE MAN

What is the source of the stereotype that women talk a lot? Dale Spender suggests that most people feel instinctively (if not consciously) that women, like children, should be seen and not heard, so any amount of talk from them seems like too much. Studies have shown that if women and men talk equally in a group, people think the women talked more. So there is truth to Spender's view. But another explanation is that men think women talk a lot because they hear women talking in situations where men would not: on the telephone; or in social situations with friends, when they are not discussing topics that men find inherently interesting; or, like the couple at the women's group, at home alone—in other words, in private speaking.

Home is the setting for an American icon that features the silent man and the talkative woman. And this icon, which grows out of the different goals and habits I have been describing, explains why the complaint most often voiced by women about the men with whom they are intimate is "He doesn't talk to me"—and the second most frequent is "He doesn't listen to me."

A woman who wrote to Ann Landers is typical:

> My husband never speaks to me when he comes home from work. When I ask, "How did everything go today?" he says, "Rough . . ." or "It's a jungle out there." (We live in Jersey and he works in New York City.)
>
> It's a different story when we have guests or go visiting. Paul is the gabbiest guy in the crowd—a real spellbinder. He comes up with the most interesting stories. People hang on every word. I think to myself, "Why doesn't he ever tell *me* these things?"
>
> This has been going on for 38 years. Paul started to go quiet on me after 10 years of marriage. I could never figure out why. Can you solve the mystery?
>
> —THE INVISIBLE WOMAN

Ann Landers suggests that the husband may not want to talk because he is tired when he comes home from work. Yet women who work come home tired too, and they are nonetheless eager to tell their partners or friends everything that happened to them during the day and what these fleeting, daily dramas made them think and feel.

Sources as lofty as studies conducted by psychologists, as down to earth as letters written to advice columnists, and as sophisticated as movies and plays come up with the same insight: Men's silence at home is a disappointment to women. Again and again, women complain, "He seems to have everything to say to everyone else, and nothing to say to me."

The film *Divorce American Style* opens with a conversation in which Debbie Reynolds is claiming that she and Dick Van Dyke don't communicate, and he is protesting that he tells her everything that's on his mind. The doorbell interrupts their quarrel, and husband and wife compose themselves before opening the door to greet their guests with cheerful smiles.

Behind closed doors, many couples are having conversations like this. Like the character played by Debbie Reynolds, women feel men don't communicate. Like the husband played by Dick Van Dyke, men feel wrongly accused. How can she be convinced that he doesn't tell her anything, while he is equally convinced he tells her everything that's on his mind? How can women and men have such different ideas about the same conversations?

When something goes wrong, people look around for a source to blame: either the person they are trying to communicate with ("You're demanding, stubborn, self-centered") or the group that the other person belongs to ("All women are demanding"; "All men are self-centered"). Some generous-minded people blame the relationship ("We just can't communicate"). But underneath, or overlaid on these types of blame cast outward, most people believe that something is wrong with them.

If individual people or particular relationships were to blame, there wouldn't be so many different people having the same problems. The real problem is conversational style. Women and men have different ways of talking. Even with the best intentions, trying to settle the problem through talk can only make things worse if it is ways of talking that are causing trouble in the first place.

BEST FRIENDS

Once again, the seeds of women's and men's styles are sown in the ways they learn to use language while growing up. In our culture, most people, but especially women, look to their closest relationships as havens in a hostile world. The center of a little girl's social life is her best friend. Girls' friendships are made and maintained by telling secrets. For grown women too, the essence of friendship is talk, telling each other what they're thinking and feeling, and what happened that day: who was at the bus stop, who called, what they said, how that made them feel. When asked who their best friends are, most women name other women they talk to regularly. When asked the same question, most men will say it's their wives. After that, many men name other men with whom they do things such as play tennis or baseball (but never just sit and talk) or a chum from high school whom they haven't spoken to in a year.

When Debbie Reynolds complained that Dick Van Dyke didn't tell her anything, and he protested that he did, both were right. She felt he didn't tell her anything because he didn't tell her the fleeting thoughts and feelings he experienced throughout the day—the kind of talk she would have with her best friend. He didn't tell her these things because to him they didn't seem like anything to tell. He told her anything that seemed important—anything he would tell his friends.

Men and women often have very different ideas of what's important—and at what point "important" topics should be raised. A woman told me, with lingering incredulity, of a conversation with her boyfriend. Knowing he had seen his friend Oliver, she asked, "What's new with Oliver?" He replied, "Nothing." But later in the conversation it came out that Oliver and his girlfriend had decided to get married. "That's nothing?" the woman gasped in frustration and disbelief.

For men, "Nothing" may be a ritual response at the start of a conversation. A college woman missed her brother but rarely called him because she found it difficult to get talk going. A typical conversation began with her asking, "What's up with you?" and his replying, "Nothing." Hearing his "Nothing" as meaning "There is nothing personal I want to talk about," she supplied talk by filling him in on her news and eventually hung up in frustration. But when she thought back, she remembered that later in the conversation he had mumbled, "Christie and I got into another fight." This came so late and so low that she didn't pick up on it. And he was probably equally frustrated that she didn't.

Many men honestly do not know what women want, and women honestly do not know why men find what they want so hard to comprehend and deliver.

DISCUSSION QUESTIONS

1. How would you summarize Tannen's characterization of gender differences in linguistic styles found in the United States?
2. Have you seen any of these gender differences in linguistic style operating in your own conversations with members of the opposite gender? Be specific.
3. Based on Tannen's description of female and male communication styles, what practical suggestions would you make to men and women in the United States to help them improve their cross-gender communication?

RESOURCES ON THE INTERNET

InfoTrac College Edition

(http://infotrac.thomsonlearning.com/index.html)

You can find further relevant readings by searching *InfoTrac College Edition,* an online library with access to thousands of scholarly and popular periodicals. Below are suggested search terms for this article:

- linguistics
- cross-cultural communication

Anthropology Online: Wadsworth's Anthropology Resource Center

(http://anthropology.wadsworth.com)

The Wadsworth Anthropology Resource Center contains a wealth of information and useful tools for students including information on careers in anthropology.

4

Eating Christmas in the Kalahari

RICHARD BORSHAY LEE

In this selection, cultural anthropologist Richard Lee recounts his experience while conducting fieldwork among the !Kung (today referred to as the Ju/'hoansi) of southwest Africa. Much to Lee's dismay, his attempt to give the local !Kung the largest and fattest oxen to slaughter and share as a Christmas feast was met with ridicule.

This is a classic example of cross-cultural misunderstanding. Lee's confusion and hurt feelings stemmed from a common mistake made by people (even anthropologists!) operating in a culturally unfamiliar environment—that is, they try to understand other peoples' behavior in terms of the assumptions of their own culture. To Lee, his gift to the community of the fattest oxen he could find was no more than a generous expression of his gratitude for their assistance and hospitality. Yet the group taunted Lee with insults about the inadequacy of the gift. Did the !Kung truly not appreciate the gift, or was there another explanation for their negative reaction?

The !Kung Bushmen's knowledge of Christmas is thirdhand. The London Missionary Society brought the holiday to the southern Tswana tribes in the early nineteenth century. Later, native catechists spread the idea far and wide among the Bantu-speaking pastoralists, even in the remotest corners of the Kalahari Desert. The Bushmen's idea of the Christmas story, stripped to its essentials, is "praise the birth of white man's god-chief"; what keeps their interest in the holiday high is the Tswana-Herero custom of slaughtering an ox for his Bushmen neighbors as an annual goodwill gesture. Since the 1930's, part of the Bushmen's annual round of activities has included a December congregation at the cattle posts for trading, marriage brokering, and several days of trance-dance feasting at which the local Tswana headman is host.

As a social anthropologist working with !Kung Bushmen, I found that the Christmas ox

Editor's note: The !Kung and other Bushmen speak click languages. In the story, three different clicks are used:

1. The dental click (/), as in /ai/ai, /ontah, and /gaugo. The click is sometimes written in English as tsk-tsk.
2. The alveopalatal click (!), as in Ben!a and !Kung.
3. The lateral click (//), as in //gom. Clicks junction as consonants; a word may have more than one, as in/n!au.

custom suited my purposes. I had come to the Kalahari to study the hunting and gathering subsistence economy of the !Kung, and to accomplish this it was essential not to provide them with food, share my own food, or interfere in any way with their food-gathering activities. While liberal handouts of tobacco and medical supplies were appreciated, they were scarcely adequate to erase the glaring disparity in wealth between the anthropologist, who maintained a two-month inventory of canned goods, and the Bushmen, who rarely had a day's supply of food on hand. My approach, while paying off in terms of data, left me open to frequent accusations of stinginess and hard-heartedness. By their lights, I was a miser.

The Christmas ox was to be my way of saying thank you for the cooperation of the past year; and since it was to be our last Christmas in the field, I determined to slaughter the largest, meatiest ox that money could buy, insuring that the feast and trance dance would be a success.

Through December I kept my eyes open at the wells as the cattle were brought down for watering. Several animals were offered, but none had quite the grossness that I had in mind. Then, ten days before the holiday, a Herero friend led an ox of astonishing size and mass up to our camp. It was solid black, stood five feet high at the shoulder, had a five-foot span of horns, and must have weighed 1,200 pounds on the hoof. Food consumption calculations are my specialty, and I quickly figured that bones and viscera aside, there was enough meat—at least four pounds—for every man, woman, and child of the 150 Bushmen in the vicinity of /ai/ai who were expected at the feast.

Having found the right animal at last, I paid the Herero £20 ($56) and asked him to keep the beast with his herd until Christmas day. The next morning word spread among the people that the big solid black one was the ox chosen by/ontah (my Bushman name; it means, roughly, "whitey") for the Christmas feast. That afternoon I received the first delegation. Ben!a, an outspoken sixty-year-old mother of five, came to the point slowly.

"Where were you planning to eat Christmas?"

"Right here at/ai/ai," I replied.

"Alone or with others?"

"I expect to invite all the people to eat Christmas with me."

"Eat what?"

"I have purchased Yehave's black ox, and I am going to slaughter and cook it."

"That's what we were told at the well but refused to believe it until we heard it from yourself."

"Well, it's the black one," I replied expansively, although wondering what she was driving at.

"Oh, no!" Ben!a groaned, turning to her group. "They were right." Turning back to me she asked, "Do you expect us to eat that bag of bones?"

"Bag of bones! It's the biggest ox at /ai/ai."

"Big, yes, but old. And thin. Everybody knows there's no meat on that old ox. What did you expect us to eat off it, the horns?"

Everybody chuckled at Ben!a's one-liner as they walked away, but all I could manage was a weak grin.

That evening it was the turn of the young men. They came to sit at our evening fire. /gaugo, about my age, spoke to me man-to-man.

"/ontah, you have always been square with us," he lied. "What has happened to change your heart? That sack of guts and bones of Yehave's will hardly feed one camp, let alone all the Bushmen around /ai/ai." And he proceeded to enumerate the seven camps in the /ai/ai vicinity, family by family. "Perhaps you have forgotten that we are not few, but many. Or are you too blind to tell the difference between a proper cow and an old wreck? That ox is thin to the point of death."

"Look, you guys," I retorted, "that is a beautiful animal, and I'm sure you will eat it with pleasure at Christmas."

"Of course we will eat it; it's food. But it won't fill us up to the point where we will have enough strength to dance. We will eat and go home to bed with stomachs rumbling."

That night as we turned in, I asked my wife Nancy: "What did you think of the black ox?"

"It looked enormous to me. Why?"

"Well, about eight different people have told me I got gypped; that the ox is nothing but bones."

"What's the angle?" Nancy asked. "Did they have a better one to sell?"

"No, they just said that it was going to be a grim Christmas because there won't be enough meat to go around. Maybe I'll get an independent judge to look at the beast in the morning."

Bright and early, Halingisi, a Tswana cattle-owner, appeared at our camp. But before I could ask him to give me his opinion on Yehave's black ox, he gave me the eye signal that indicated a confidential chat. We left the camp and sat down.

"/ontah, I'm surprised at you; you've lived here for three years and still haven't learned anything about cattle."

"But what else can a person do but choose the biggest, strongest animal one can find?" I retorted.

"Look, just because an animal is big doesn't mean that it has plenty of meat on it. The black one was a beauty when it was younger, but now it is thin to the point of death."

"Well, I've already bought it. What can I do at this stage?"

"Bought it already? I thought you were just considering it. Well, you'll have to kill it and serve it, I suppose. But don't expect much of a dance to follow."

My spirits dropped rapidly. I could believe that Ben!a and /gaugo just might be putting me on about the black ox, but Halingisi seemed to be an impartial critic. I went around that day feeling as though I had bought a lemon of a used car.

In the afternoon it was Tomazo's turn. Tomazo is a fine hunter, a top trance performer, and one of most reliable informants. He approached the subject of the Christmas cow as part of my continuing Bushman education.

"My friend, the way it is with us Bushmen," he began, "is that we love meat. And even more than that, we love fat. When we hunt we always search for the fat ones, the ones dripping with layers of white fat: fat that turns into a clear, thick oil in the cooking pot, fat that slides down your gullet, fills your stomach and gives you a roaring diarrhea," he rhapsodized.

"So, feeling as we do," he continued, "it gives us pain to be served such a scrawny thing as Yehave's black ox. It is big, yes, and no doubt its giant bones are good for soup, but fat is what we really crave and so we will eat Christmas this year with a heavy heart."

The prospect of a gloomy Christmas now had me worried, so I asked Tomazo what I could do about it.

"Look for a fat one, a young one . . . smaller, but fat. Fat enough to make us / /*gom* ('evacuate the bowels'), then we will be happy."

My suspicions were aroused when Tomazo said that he happened to know of a young, fat, barren cow that the owner was willing to part with. Was Toma working on commission, I wondered? But I dispelled this unworthy thought when we approached the Herero owner of the cow in question and found that he had decided not to sell.

The scrawny wreck of a Christmas ox now became the talk of the /ai/ai water hole and was the first news told to the outlying groups as they began to come in from the bush for the feast. What finally convinced me that real trouble might be brewing was the visit from u!au, an old conservative with a reputation for fierceness. His nickname meant spear and referred to an incident thirty years ago in which he had speared a man to death. He had an intense manner; fixing me with his eyes, he said in clipped tones:

"I have only just heard about the black ox today, or else I would have come here earlier. /ontah, do you honestly think you can serve meat like that to people and avoid a fight?" He paused, letting the implications sink in. "I don't mean fight you, /ontah; you are a white man. I mean a fight between Bushmen. There are many fierce ones here, and with such a small quantity of meat to distribute, how can you give everybody a fair share? Someone is sure to accuse another of taking too much or hogging all the choice pieces. Then you will see what happens when some go hungry while others eat."

The possibility of at least a serious argument struck me as all too real. I had witnessed the tension that surrounds the distribution of meat from a kudu or gemsbok kill, and had documented many arguments that sprang up from a real or imagined slight in meat distribution. The owners of a kill may spend up to two hours arranging and rearranging the piles of meat under the gaze of a circle of recipients before handing them out. And I also knew that the Christmas feast at /ai/ai would be bringing together groups that had feuded in the past.

Convinced now of the gravity of the situation, I went in earnest to search for a second cow; but all my inquiries failed to turn one up.

The Christmas feast was evidently going to be a disaster, and the incessant complaints about the meagerness of the ox had already taken the fun out of it for me. Moreover, I was getting bored with the wisecracks, and after losing my temper a few times, I resolved to serve the beast anyway. If the meat fell short, the hell with it. In the Bushmen idiom, I announced to all who would listen:

"I am a poor man and blind. If I have chosen one that is too old and too thin, we will eat it anyway and see if there is enough meat there to quiet the rumbling of our stomachs."

On hearing this speech, Ben!a offered me a rare word of comfort. "It's thin," she said philosophically, "but the bones will make a good soup."

At dawn Christmas morning, instinct told me to turn over the butchering and cooking to a friend and take off with Nancy to spend Christmas alone in the bush. But curiosity kept me from retreating. I wanted to see what such a scrawny ox looked like on butchering, and if there *was* going to be a fight, I wanted to catch every word of it. Anthropologists are incurable that way.

The great beast was driven up to our dancing ground, and a shot in the forehead dropped it in its tracks. Then, freshly cut branches were heaped around the fallen carcass to receive the meat. Ten men volunteered to help with the cutting. I asked /gaugo to make the breast bone cut. This cut, which begins the butchering process for most large game, offers easy access for removal of the viscera. But it also allows the hunter to spot-check the amount of fat on the animal. A fat game animal carries a white layer up to an inch thick on the chest, while in a thin one, the knife will quickly cut to bone. All eyes fixed on his hand as /gaugo, dwarfed by the great carcass, knelt to the breast. The first cut opened a pool of solid white in the black skin. The second and third cut widened and deepened the creamy white. Still no bone. It was pure fat; it must have been two inches thick.

"Hey /gau," I burst out, "that ox is loaded with fat. What's this about the ox being too thin to bother eating? Are you out of your mind?"

"Fat?" /gau shot back, "You call that fat? This wreck is thin, sick, dead!" And he broke out laughing. So did everyone else. They rolled on the ground, paralyzed with laughter. Everybody laughed except me; I was thinking.

I ran back to the tent and burst in just as Nancy was getting up. "Hey, the black ox. It's fat as hell! They were kidding about it being too thin to eat. It was a joke or something. A put-on. Everyone is really delighted with it!"

"Some joke," my wife replied. "It was so funny that you were ready to pack up and leave /ai/ai."

If it had indeed been a joke, it had been an extraordinarily convincing one, and tinged, I thought, with more than a touch of malice as many jokes are. Nevertheless, that it was a joke lifted my spirits considerably, and I returned to the butchering site where the shape of the ox was rapidly disappearing under the axes and knives of the butchers. The atmosphere had become festive. Grinning broadly, their arms covered with blood well past the elbow, men packed chunks of meat into the big cast-iron cooking pots, fifty pounds to the load, and muttered and chuckled all the while about the thinness and worthlessness of the animal and /ontah's poor judgment.

We danced and ate that ox two days and two nights; we cooked and distributed fourteen potfuls of meat and no one went home hungry and no fights broke out.

But the "joke" stayed in my mind. I had a growing feeling that something important had happened in my relationship with the Bushmen and that the clue lay in the meaning of the joke. Several days later, when most of the people had dispersed back to the bush camps, I raised the question with Hakekgose, a Tswana man who had grown up among the !Kung, married a !Kung girl, and who probably knew their culture better than any other non-Bushman.

"With us whites," I began, "Christmas is supposed to be the day of friendship and brotherly love. What I can't figure out is why the Bushmen went to such lengths to criticize and belittle the ox I had bought for the feast. The animal was perfectly good and their jokes and wisecracks practically ruined the holiday for me."

"So it really did bother you," said Hakekgose. "Well, that's the way they always talk. When I take my rifle and go hunting with them, if I miss, they laugh at me for the rest of the day. But even if I hit and bring one down, it's no better. To them, the kill is always too small or too old or too thin; and as we sit down on the kill site to cook and eat the liver, they keep grumbling, even with their mouths full of meat. They say things like, 'Oh this is awful! What a worthless animal! Whatever made me think that this Tswana rascal could hunt!' "

"Is this the way outsiders are treated?" I asked.

"No, it is their custom; they talk that way to each other too. Go and ask them."

/gaugo had been one of the most enthusiastic in making me feel bad about the merit of the Christmas ox. I sought him out first.

"Why did you tell me the black ox was worthless, when you could see that it was loaded with fat and meat?"

"It is our way," he said smiling. "We always like to fool people about that. Say there is a Bushman who has been hunting. He must not come home and announce like a braggard, 'I have killed a big one in the bush!' He must first sit down in silence until I or someone else comes up to his fire and asks, 'What did you see today?' He replies quietly, 'Ah, I'm no good for hunting. I saw nothing at all [pause] just a little tiny one.' Then I smile to myself," /gaugo continued, "because I know he has killed something big.

"In the morning we make up a party of four or five people to cut up and carry the meat back to the camp. When we arrive at the kill we examine it and cry out, 'You mean to say you have dragged us all the way out here in order to make us cart home your pile of bones? Oh, if I had known it was this thin I wouldn't have come.' Another one pipes up, 'People, to think I gave up a nice day in the shade for this. At home we may be hungry but at least we have nice cool water to drink.' If the horns are big, someone says, 'Did you think that somehow you were going to boil down the horns for soup?'

"To all this you must respond in kind. 'I agree,' you say, 'this one is not worth the effort; let's just cook the liver for strength and leave the rest for the hyenas. It is not too late to hunt today and even a duiker or a steenbok would be better than this mess.'

"Then you set to work nevertheless; butcher the animal, carry the meat back to the camp and everyone eats," /gaugo concluded.

Things were beginning to make sense. Next, I went to Tomazo. He corroborated /gaugo's story of the obligatory insults over a kill and added a few details of his own.

"But," I asked, "why insult a man after he has gone to all that trouble to track and kill an animal and when he is going to share the meat with you so that your children will have something to eat?"

"Arrogance." was his cryptic answer.

"Arrogance?"

"Yes, when a young man kills much meat he comes to think of himself as a chief or a big man, and he thinks of the rest of us as his servants or inferiors. We can't accept this. We refuse one who boasts, for someday his pride will make him kill somebody. So we always speak of his meat as worthless. This way we cool his heart and make him gentle."

"But why didn't you tell me this before?" I asked Tomazo with some heat.

"Because you never asked me," said Tomazo, echoing the refrain that has come to haunt every field ethnographer.

The pieces now fell into place. I had known for a long time that in situations of social conflict with Bushmen I held all the cards. I was the only source of tobacco in a thousand square miles, and I was not incapable of cutting an individual off for noncooperation. Though my boycott never lasted longer than a few days, it was an indication of my strength. People resented my presence at the water hole, yet simultaneously dreaded my leaving. In short I was a perfect target for the charge of arrogance and for the Bushmen tactic of enforcing humility.

I had been taught an object lesson by the Bushmen; it had come from an unexpected corner and had hurt me in a vulnerable area. For the big black ox was to be the one totally generous, unstinting act of my year at /ai/ai, and I was quite unprepared for the reaction I received.

As I read it, their message was this: There are no totally generous acts. All "acts" have an element of calculation. One black ox slaughtered at Christmas does not wipe out a year of careful manipulation of gifts given to serve your own ends. After all, to kill an animal and share the meat with people is really no more than Bushmen do for each other every day and with far less fanfare.

In the end, I had to admire how the Bushmen had played out the farce—collectively straight-faced to the end. Curiously, the episode reminded me of the *Good Soldier Schweik* and his marvelous encounters with authority. Like Schweik, the Bushmen had retained a thoroughgoing skepticism of good intentions. Was it this independence of spirit, I wondered, that had kept them culturally viable in the face of generations of contact with more powerful societies, both black and white? The thought that the Bushmen were alive and well in the Kalahari was strangely comforting. Perhaps, armed with that independence and with their superb knowledge of their environment, they might yet survive the future.

DISCUSSION QUESTIONS

1. How would you explain the misunderstanding that occurred between Lee and the !Kung concerning the gift of the oxen?
2. Why was Lee a particularly good candidate for charges of arrogance?
3. What general principle about cross-cultural understanding does this story exemplify?

RESOURCES ON THE INTERNET

InfoTrac College Edition

(http://infotrac.thomsonlearning.com/index.html)

You can find further relevant readings by searching *InfoTrac College Edition,* an online library with access to thousands of scholarly and popular periodicals. Below are suggested search terms for this article:

- arrogance
- humility
- farce

Anthropology Online: Wadsworth's Anthropology Resource Center

(http://anthropology.wadsworth.com)

The Wadsworth Anthropology Resource Center contains a wealth of information and useful tools for students including information on careers in anthropology.

5

The Potlatch

MARVIN HARRIS

Franz Boas, the father of anthropology in the United States, was one of the first to study the practice of the potlatch. On the face of it, the potlatch would appear to be a bizarre, if not irrational, cultural practice. As practiced by the Kwakuitl and other Native American groups in British Columbia, the potlatch is a form of competitive feasting which involves giving away or destroying more material wealth (e.g., food, clothing, and blankets) than one's rival. Since the original description of this practice by Boas in the late nineteenth century, the potlatch has been cited often as an excellent example of conspicuous consumption gone berserk, or at least an irrational practice. By taking a materialist interpretation rather than a psychological one, Harris suggests that the potlatch is more than just an insane pursuit of social status. Instead, Harris sees the potlatch as a rational response to economic and social forces. While not denying that the potlatch involves fierce competition for status and prestige, it also serves a number of other important functions which contribute to the overall well-being of the society, not the least of which is as a mechanism of economic distribution.

Some of the most puzzling lifestyles on exhibit in the museum of world ethnography bear the imprint of a strange craving known as the "drive for prestige." Some people seem to hunger for approval as others hunger for meat. The puzzling thing is not that people hunger for approval, but that occasionally their craving seems to become so powerful that they begin to compete with each other for prestige as others compete for land or protein or sex. Sometimes this competition grows so fierce that it appears to become an end in itself. It then takes on the appearance of an obsession wholly divorced from, and even directly opposed to, rational calculations of material costs.

Vance Packard struck a responsive chord when he described the United States as a nation of competitive status seekers. Many Americans seem to spend their entire lives trying to climb further up the social pyramid simply in order to impress each other. We seem to be more interested in working in order to get people to admire us for our wealth than in the actual wealth itself, which often enough consists of chromium baubles and burdensome or useless objects. It is amazing how much effort people are willing to spend to obtain what Thorstein Veblen described as the vicarious thrill of being mistaken for members of a class that doesn't have to work. Veblen's mordant phrases "conspicuous consumption" and "conspicuous waste" aptly convey a sense of the peculiarly intense desire for "keeping up with the Joneses" that lies behind the ceaseless cosmetic alterations in the automotive, appliance, and clothing industries.

Early in the present century, anthropologists were surprised to discover that certain primitive tribes engaged in conspicuous consumption and conspicuous waste to a degree unmatched by even the most wasteful of modern consumer economies. Ambitious, status-hungry men were found competing with each other for approval by giving huge feasts. The rival feast givers judged each other by the amount of food they provided, and a feast was a success only if the guests could eat until they were stupefied, stagger off into the bush, stick their fingers down their throats, vomit, and come back for more.

The most bizarre instance of status seeking was discovered among the American Indians who formerly inhabited the coastal regions of Southern Alaska, British Columbia, and Washington. Here the status seekers practiced what seems like a maniacal form of conspicuous consumption and conspicuous waste known as *potlatch*. The object of potlatch was to give away or destroy more wealth than one's rival. If the potlatch giver was a powerful chief, he might attempt to shame his rivals and gain everlasting admiration from his followers by destroying food, clothing, and money. Sometimes he might even seek prestige by burning down his own house.

Potlatch was made famous by Ruth Benedict in her book *Patterns of Culture,* which describes how potlatch operated among the Kwakiutl, the aboriginal inhabitants of Vancouver Island. Benedict thought that potlatch was part of a megalomaniacal lifestyle characteristic of Kwakiutl culture in general. It was the "cup" God had given them to drink from. Ever since, potlatch has been a monument to the belief that cultures are the creations of inscrutable forces and deranged personalities. As a result of reading *Patterns of Culture,* experts in many fields concluded that the drive for prestige makes a shambles of attempts to explain lifestyles in terms of practical and mundane factors.

I want to show here that the Kwakiutl potlatch was not the result of maniacal whims, but of definite economic and ecological conditions. When these conditions are absent, the need to be admired and the drive for prestige express themselves in completely different lifestyle practices. Inconspicuous consumption replaces conspicuous consumption, conspicuous waste is forbidden, and there are no competitive status seekers.

The Kwakiutl used to live in plank-house villages set close to the shore in the midst of cedar and fir rain forests. They fished and hunted along the island-studded sounds and fiords of Vancouver in huge dugout canoes. Always eager to attract traders, they made their villages conspicuous by erecting on the beach the carved tree trunks we erroneously call "totem poles." The carvings on these poles symbolized the ancestral titles to which the chiefs of the village laid claim.

A Kwakiutl chief was never content with the amount of respect he was getting from his own followers and from neighboring chiefs. He was always insecure about his status. True enough, the family titles to which he laid claim belonged to his ancestors. But there were other people who could trace descent from the same ancestors and who were entitled to vie with him for recognition as a chief. Every chief therefore felt the obligation to justify and validate his chiefly pretensions. The prescribed manner for doing this was to hold potlatches. Each potlatch was given by a host chief and his followers to a guest chief and his followers. The object of the potlatch was to show that the host chief was truly entitled to chiefly status and that he was more exalted than the guest chief. To prove this point, the host chief gave the rival chief and his followers quantities of valuable gifts. The guests would belittle what they received and vow to hold a return potlatch at which their own chief would prove that he was greater than the former host by giving back even larger quantities of more valuable gifts.

Preparations for potlatch required the accumulation of fresh and dried fish, fish oil, berries, animal skins, blankets, and other valuables. On the appointed day, the guests paddled up to the host village and went into the chiefs house. There they gorged themselves on salmon and wild berries while dancers masked as beaver gods and thunderbirds entertained them.

The host chief and his followers arranged in neat piles the wealth that was to be given away. The visitors stared at their host sullenly as he pranced up and down, boasting about how much he was about to give them. As he counted out the boxes of fish oil, baskets full of berries, and piles of blankets, he commented derisively on the poverty of his rivals. Laden with gifts, the guests finally were free to paddle back to their own village. Stung to the quick, the guest chief and his followers vowed to get even. This could only be achieved by inviting their rivals to a return potlatch and obliging them to accept even greater amounts of valuables than they had given away. Considering all the Kwakiutl villages as a single unit, potlatch stimulated a ceaseless flow of prestige and valuables moving in opposite directions.

An ambitious chief and his followers had potlatch rivals in several different villages at once. Specialists in counting property kept track of what had to be done in each village in order to even the score. If a chief managed to get the better of his rivals in one place, he still had to confront his adversaries in another.

At the potlatch, the host chief would say things like, "I am the only great tree. Bring your counter of property that he may try in vain to count the property that is to be given away." Then the chief's followers demanded silence from the guests with the warning: "Do not make any noise, tribes. Be quiet or we shall cause a landslide of wealth from our chief, the overhanging mountain." At some potlatches blankets and other valuables were not given away but were destroyed. Sometimes successful potlatch chiefs decided to hold "grease feasts" at which boxes of oil obtained from the candlefish were poured on the fire in the center of the house. As the flames roared up, dark grease smoke filled the room. The guests sat impassively or even complained about the chill in the air while the wealth destroyer ranted, "I am the only one on earth—the only one in the whole world who makes this smoke rise from the beginning of the year to the end for the invited tribes." At some grease feasts the flames ignited the planks in the roof and an entire house would become a potlatch offering, causing the greatest shame to the guests and much rejoicing among the hosts.

According to Ruth Benedict, potlatching was caused by the obsessive status hunger of the Kwakiutl chiefs. "Judged by the standards of other cultures the speeches of their chiefs are unabashed megalomania," she wrote. "The object of all Kwakiutl enterprises was to show oneself superior to one's rivals." In her opinion, the whole aboriginal economic system of the Pacific Northwest was "bent to the service of this obsession."

I think that Benedict was mistaken. The economic system of the Kwakiutl was not bent to the service of status rivalry; rather, status rivalry was bent to the service of the economic system.

All of the basic ingredients of the Kwakiutl giveaways, except for their destructive aspects, are present in primitive societies widely dispersed over different parts of the globe. Stripped down to its elementary core, the potlatch is a competitive feast, a nearly universal mechanism for assuring the production and distribution of wealth among peoples who have not yet fully acquired a ruling class.

Melanesia and New Guinea present the best opportunity to study competitive feasting under relatively pristine conditions. Throughout this region, there are so-called big men who owe their superior status to the large number of feasts that each has sponsored during his lifetime. Each feast has to be preceded by an intensive effort on the part of an aspiring big man to accumulate the necessary wealth.

Among the Kaoka-speaking people of the Solomon Islands, for example, the status-hungry individual begins his career by making his wife and children plant larger yam gardens. As described by the Australian anthropologist Ian Hogbin, the Kaoka who wants to become a big man then gets his kinsmen and his age-mates to help him fish. Later he begs sows from his friends and increases the size of his pig herd. As the litters are born he boards additional animals among his neighbors. Soon his relatives and friends feel that the young man is going to be a success. They see his large gardens and his big pig herd and they redouble their own efforts to make the forthcoming feast a memorable one. When he becomes a big man they want the young candidate to remember that they helped him. Finally, they all get together and build an extra-fine house. The men go off on one last fishing expedition. The women harvest yams and collect firewood, banana leaves, and coconuts. As the guests arrive (as in the ease of potlatch), the wealth is stacked in neat piles and put on display for everyone to count and admire.

On the day of the feast given by a young man named Atana, Hogbin counted the following items: 250 pounds of dried fish, 3,000 yam and coconut cakes, 11 large bowls of yam pudding, and 8 pigs. All this was the direct result of the extra work effort organized by Atana. But some of the guests themselves, anticipating an important occasion, brought presents to be added to the giveaway. Their contributions raised the total to 300 pounds of fish, 5,000 cakes, 19 bowls of pudding and 13 pigs. Atana proceeded to divide this wealth into 257 portions, one each for every person who had helped him or who had brought gifts, rewarding some more than others. "Only the remnants were left for Atana himself," notes Hogbin. This is normal for status seekers in Guadalcanal, who always say: "The giver of the feast takes the bones and the stale cakes; the meat and the fat go to the others."

The feast-giving days of the big man, like those of the potlatch chiefs, are never over. On threat of being reduced to commoner status, each big man is obliged to busy himself with plans and preparations for the next feast. Since there are several big men per village and community, these plans and preparations often lead to complex competitive maneuvering for the allegiance of relatives and neighbors. The big men work harder, worry more, and consume less than anybody else. Prestige is their only reward.

The big man can be described as a worker-entrepreneur—the Russians call them "Stakhanovites"—who renders important services to society by raising the level of production. As a result of the big man's craving for status, more people work harder and produce more food and other valuables.

Under conditions where everyone has equal access to the means of subsistence, competitive feasting serves the practical function of preventing the labor force from falling back to levels of productivity that offer no margin of safety in crises such as war and crop failures. Furthermore, since there are no formal political institutions capable of integrating independent villages into a common economic framework competitive feasting creates an extensive network of economic expectations. This has the effect of pooling the productive effort of larger populations than can be mobilized by any given village. Finally, competitive feasting by big men acts as an automatic equalizer of annual fluctuations in productivity among a series of villages that occupy different microenvironments—seacoast, lagoon, or upland habitats. Automatically, the biggest feasts in any given year will be hosted by villages that have enjoyed conditions of rainfall, temperature, and humidity most favorable to production.

All of these points apply to the Kwakiutl. The Kwakiutl chiefs were like Melanesian big men except that they operated with a much more productive technological inventory in a richer environment. Like big men, they competed with each other to attract men and women to their villages. The greatest chiefs were the best providers and gave the biggest potlatches. The chief's followers shared vicariously in his prestige and helped him to achieve more exalted honors. The chiefs commissioned the carving of the "totem poles." These were in fact grandiose advertisements proclaiming by their height and bold designs that here was a village with a mighty chief who could cause great works to be done, and who could protect his followers from famine and disease. In claiming hereditary rights to the animal crests carved on the poles, the chiefs were actually saying that they were great providers of food and comfort. Potlatch was a means of telling their rivals to put up or shut up.

Despite the overt competitive thrust of potlatch, it functioned aboriginally to transfer food and other valuables from centers of high productivity to less fortunate villages. I should put this even more strongly: Because of the competitive thrust, such transfers were assured. Since there were unpredictable fluctuations in fish runs, wild fruit and vegetable harvests, intervillage potlatching was advantageous from the standpoint of the regional population as a whole. When the fish spawned in nearby streams and the berries ripened close at hand, last year's guests became this year's hosts. Aboriginally, potlatch meant that each year the haves gave and the have-nots took. To eat, all a have-not had to do was admit that the rival chief was a great man.

Why did the practical basis of potlatch escape the attention of Ruth Benedict? Anthropologists began to study potlatch only long after the aboriginal peoples of the Pacific Northwest had entered into commercial and wage-labor relations with Russian, English, Canadian, and American merchants and settlers. This contact rapidly gave rise to epidemics of smallpox and other European diseases that killed off a large part of the native population. For example, the population of the Kwakiutl fell from 23,000 in 1836 to 2,000 in 1886. The decline automatically intensified the competition for manpower. At the same time, wages paid by the Europeans pumped unprecedented amounts of wealth into the potlatch network. From the Hudson's Bay Company, the Kwakiutl received thousands of trade blankets in exchange for animal skins. At the great potlatches these blankets replaced food as the most important item to be given away. The dwindling population soon found itself with more blankets and other valuables than it could consume. Yet the need to attract followers was greater than ever due to the labor shortage. So the potlatch chiefs ordered the destruction of property in the vain hope that such spectacular demonstrations of wealth would bring the people back to the empty villages. But these were the practices of a dying culture struggling to adapt to a new set of political and economic conditions; they bore little resemblance to the potlatch of aboriginal times.

Competitive feasting thought about, narrated, and imagined by the participants is very different from competitive feasting viewed as an adaptation to material constraints and opportunities. In the social dreamwork—the lifestyle consciousness of the participants—competitive feasting is a manifestation of the big man's or potlatch chief's insatiable craving for prestige. But from the point of view followed in this book, the insatiable craving for prestige is a manifestation of competitive feasting. Every society makes use of the need for approval, but not every society links prestige to success in competitive feasting.

Competitive feasting as a source of prestige must be seen in evolutionary perspective to be properly understood. Big men like Atana or the Kwakiutl chiefs carry out a form of economic exchange known as redistribution. That is, they gather together the results of the productive effort of many individuals and then redistribute the aggregated wealth in different quantities to a different set of people. As I have said, the Kaoka redistributor-big man works harder, worries more, and consumes less than anybody else in the village. This is not true of the Kwakiutl chief-redistributor. The great potlatch chiefs performed the entrepreneurial and managerial functions that were necessary for a big potlatch, but aside from an occasional fishing or sea-lion expedition, they left the hardest work to their followers. The greatest potlatch chiefs even had a few war captives working for them as slaves. From the point of view of consumption privileges, the Kwakiutl chiefs had begun to reverse the Kaoka formula and were keeping some of the "meat and fat" for themselves, leaving most of the "bones and stale cakes" for their followers.

Continuing along the evolutionary line leading from Atana, the impoverished worker-entrepreneur big man, to the semihereditary Kwakiutl chiefs, we end up with state-level societies ruled over by hereditary kings who perform no basic industrial or agricultural labor and who keep the most and best of everything for themselves. At the imperial level, exalted divine-right rulers maintain their prestige by building conspicuous palaces, temples, and mega-monuments, and validate their right to hereditary privileges against all challengers—not by potlatch, but by force of arms. Reversing direction, we can go from kings to potlatch chiefs to big men, back to egalitarian lifestyles in which all competitive displays and conspicuous consumption by individuals disappear, and anyone foolish enough to boast about how great he is gets accused of witchcraft and is stoned to death.

In the truly egalitarian societies that have survived long enough to be studied by anthropologists, redistribution in the form of competitive feasting does not occur. Instead, the mode of exchange known as reciprocity predominates. Reciprocity is the technical term for an economic exchange that takes place between two individuals in which neither specifies precisely what is expected in return nor when they expect it. Superficially, reciprocal exchanges don't look like exchanges at all. The expectation of one party and obligation of the other remain unstated. One party can continue to take from the other for quite a while with no resistance from the giver and no embarrassment in the taker. Nonetheless, the transaction cannot be considered a pure gift. There is an underlying expectation of return, and if the balance between two individuals gets too far out of line, eventually the giver will start to grumble and gossip. Concern will be shown for the taker's health and sanity, and if the situation does not improve, people begin to suspect that the taker is possessed by malevolent spirits or is practicing witchcraft. In egalitarian societies, individuals who consistently violate the rules of reciprocity are in fact likely to be psychotic and a menace to their community.

We can get some idea of what reciprocal exchanges are like by thinking about the way we exchange goods and services with our close friends or relatives. Brothers, for example, are not supposed to calculate the precise dollar value of everything they do for each other. They should feel free to borrow each other's shirts or phonograph albums and ought not to hesitate to ask for favors. In brotherhood and friendship both parties accept the principle that if one has to give more than he takes, it will not affect the solidary relationship between them. If one friend invites another to dinner, there should be no hesitation in giving or accepting a second or a third invitation even if the first dinner still remains unreciprocated. Yet there is a limit to that sort of thing, because after a while unreciprocated gift-giving begins to feel suspiciously like exploitation. In other words, everybody likes to be thought generous, but nobody wants to be taken for a sucker. This is precisely the quandary we get ourselves into at Christmas when we attempt to revert to the principle of reciprocity in drawing up our shopping lists. The gift can neither be too cheap nor too expensive; and yet our calculations must appear entirely casual, so we remove the price tag.

But to really see reciprocity in action you must live in an egalitarian society that doesn't have money and where nothing can be bought or sold. Everything about reciprocity is opposed to precise counting and reckoning of what one person owes to another. In fact, the whole idea is to deny that anybody really owes anything. One can tell if a lifestyle is based on reciprocity or something else by whether or not people say thank you. In truly egalitarian societies, it is rude to be openly grateful for the receipt of material goods or services. Among the Semai of central Malaya, for example, no one ever expresses gratitude for the meat that a hunter gives away in exactly equal portions to his companions. Robert Dentan, who has lived with the Semai, found that to say thank you was very rude because it suggested either that you were calculating the size of the piece of meat you had been given, or that you were surprised by the success and generosity of the hunter.

In contrast to the conspicuous display put on by the Kaoka big man, and the boastful ranting of potlatch chiefs, and our own flaunting of status symbols, the Semai follow a lifestyle in which those who are most successful must be the least conspicuous. In their egalitarian lifestyle, status seeking through rivalrous redistribution or any form of conspicuous consumption or conspicuous waste is literally unthinkable. Egalitarian peoples are repelled and frightened by the faintest suggestion that they are being treated generously or that one person thinks he's better than another.

Professor Richard Lee of the University of Toronto tells an amusing story about the meaning of reciprocal exchange among egalitarian hunters and gatherers. For the better part of a year, Lee had been following the Bushmen around the Kalahari Desert observing what they ate. The Bushmen were very cooperative and Lee wanted to show his gratitude, but he had nothing to give them that would not disturb their normal diet and pattern of activity. As Christmas approached he learned that the Bushmen were likely to camp at the edge of the desert near villages from which they sometimes obtained meat through trade. With the intention of giving them an ox for a Christmas present, he drove about in his jeep from one village to another, trying to find the biggest ox that he could buy. In a remote village, Lee finally located an animal of monstrous proportions, one covered with a thick layer of fat. Like many primitive peoples, the Bushmen crave fatty meat because the animals they obtain by hunting are usually lean and stringy. Returning to camp, Lee took his Bushmen friends aside and told them one by one that he had bought the largest ox he had ever seen and that he was going to let them slaughter it at Christmas time.

The first man to hear the good news became visibly alarmed. He asked Leo where he had bought the ox, what color it was, and what size its horns were, and then he shook his head. "I know that ox," he said. "Why, it is nothing but skin and bones! You must have been drunk to buy such a worthless animal!" Convinced that his friend didn't really know what ox he was talking about, Lee confided in several other Bushmen, but continued to meet with the same astonished reaction: "You bought that worthless animal? Of course we will eat it," each would say, "but it won't fill us up. We will eat and go home to bed with stomachs rumbling." When Christmas came and the ox was finally slaughtered, the beast turned out to be covered with a thick layer of fat, and it was devoured with great gusto. There was more than enough meat and fat for everybody. Lee went over to his friends and insisted upon an explanation. "Yes, of course we knew all along what the ox was really like," one hunter admitted. "But when a young man kills much meat he comes to think of himself as a chief or big man, and he thinks of the rest of us as his servants or inferiors. We cannot accept this," he went on. "We refuse one who boasts, for someday his pride will make him kill somebody. So we always speak of his meat as worthless. This way we cool his heart and make him gentle."

The Eskimos explained their fear of boastful and generous gift-givers with the proverb "Gifts make slaves just as whips make dogs." And that is exactly what happened. In evolutionary perspective, the gift-givers at first gave gifts that came from their own extra work; soon people found themselves working harder to reciprocate and to make it possible for the gift-givers to give them more gifts; eventually the gift-givers became very powerful, and they no longer needed to obey the rules of reciprocity. They could force people to pay taxes and to work for them without actually redistributing what was in their storehouses and palaces. Of course, as assorted modern big men and politicians occasionally recognize, it is still easier to get "slaves" to work for you if you give them an occasional big feast instead of whipping them all the time.

If people like the Eskimo, Bushmen, and Semai understood the dangers of gift-giving, why did others permit the gift-givers to flourish? And why were big men permitted to get so puffed up that they could turn around and enslave the very people whose work made their glow possible? Once again, I suspect that I am on the verge of trying to explain everything at once. But permit me to make a few suggestions.

Reciprocity is a form of economic exchange that is primarily adapted to conditions in which the stimulation of intensive extra productive effort would have an adverse effect upon group survival. These conditions are found among certain hunters and gatherers such as the Eskimo, Semai, and Bushmen, whose survival depends entirely on the vigor of the natural communities of plants and animals in their habitat. If hunters suddenly engage in a concerted effort to capture more animals and uproot more plants, they risk permanently impairing the supply of game in their territory.

Lee found, for example, that his Bushmen worked at subsistence for only ten to fifteen hours a week. This discovery effectively destroys one of the shoddiest myths of industrial society—namely that we have more leisure today than ever before. Primitive hunters and gatherers work less than we do—without benefit of a single labor union—because their ecosystems cannot tolerate weeks and months of intensive extra effort. Among the Bushmen, Stakhanovite personalities who would run about getting friends and relatives to work harder by promising them a big feast would constitute a definite menace to society. If he got his followers to work like the Kaoka for a month, an aspiring Bushman big man would kill or scare off every game animal for miles around and starve his people to death before the end of the year. So reciprocity and not redistribution predominates among the Bushmen, and the highest prestige falls to the quietly dependable hunter who never boasts about his achievements and who avoids any hint that he is giving a gift when he divides up an animal he has killed.

Competitive feasting and other forms of redistribution overwhelmed the primordial reliance upon reciprocity when it became possible to increase the duration and intensity of work without inflicting irreversible damage upon the habitats carrying capacity. Typically this became possible when domesticated plants and animals were substituted for natural food resources. Within broad limits, the more work you put into planting and raising domesticated species, the more food you can produce. The only hitch is that people don't usually work harder than they have to. Redistribution was the answer to this problem. Redistribution began to appear as people worked harder in order to maintain a reciprocal balance with prestige-hungry, overzealous producers. As the reciprocal exchanges became unbalanced, they became gifts; and as the gifts piled up, the gift-givers were rewarded with prestige and counter-gifts. Soon redistribution predominated over reciprocity and highest prestige went to the most boastful, calculating gift-givers, who cajoled, shamed, and ultimately forced everybody to work harder than the Bushman ever dreamed was possible.

As the example of the Kwakiutl indicates, conditions appropriate for the development of competitive feasting and redistribution sometimes also occurred among nonagricultural populations. Among the coastal peoples of the Pacific Northwest, annual runs of salmon, other migratory fish, and sea mammals provided the ecological analogue of agricultural harvests. The salmon or candlefish ran in such vast numbers that if people worked harder they could always catch more fish. Moreover, as long as they fished with the aboriginal dip net, they could never catch enough fish to influence the spawning runs and deplete next year's supply.

Stepping away for the moment from our examination of reciprocal and redistributive prestige systems, we can surmise that every major type of political and economic system uses prestige in a distinctive manner. For example, with the appearance of capitalism in Western Europe, competitive acquisition of wealth once more became the fundamental criterion for big-man status. Only in this case, the big men tried to take away each other's wealth, and highest prestige and power went to the individual who managed to accumulate and hold onto the greatest fortune. During the early years of capitalism, highest prestige went to those who were richest but lived most frugally. After their fortunes had become more secure, the capitalist upper class resorted to grand-scale conspicuous consumption and conspicuous waste in order to impress their rivals. They built great mansions, dressed in exclusive finery, adorned themselves with huge jewels, and spoke contemptuously of the impoverished masses. Meanwhile, the middle and lower classes continued to award highest prestige to those who worked hardest, spent least, and soberly resisted all forms of conspicuous consumption and conspicuous waste. But as the growth of industrial capacity began to saturate the consumer market, the middle and lower classes had to be weaned away from their frugal habits. Advertising and mass media joined forces to induce the middle and lower classes to stop saving and to buy, consume, waste, destroy, or otherwise get rid of ever-larger quantities of goods and services. And so among middle-class status seekers, highest prestige now goes to the biggest and most conspicuous consumer.

But in the meantime, the rich found themselves threatened by new forms of taxation aimed at redistributing their wealth. Conspicuous consumption in the grand manner became dangerous, so highest prestige now once again goes to those who have most but show least. With the most prestigious members of the upper class no longer flaunting their wealth, some of the pressure on the middle class to engage in conspicuous consumption has also been removed. This suggests to me that the wearing of torn jeans and the rejection of overt consumerism among middle-class youth of late has more to do with aping the trends set by the upper class than with any so-called cultural revolution.

One final point. As I have shown, the replacement of reciprocity by competitive status seeking made it possible for larger human populations to survive and prosper in a given region. One might very well wish to question the sanity of the whole process by which mankind was tricked and cajoled into working harder in order to feed more people at substantially the same or even lower levels of material well-being than that enjoyed by people like the Eskimo or Bushmen. The only answer that I see to such a challenge is that many primitive societies refused to expand their productive effort and failed to increase their population density precisely because they discovered that the new "labor-saving" technologies actually meant that they would have to work harder as well as suffer a loss in living standards. But the fate of these primitive people was sealed as soon as any one of them—no matter how remotely situated—crossed the threshold to redistribution and the full-scale stratification of classes that lay beyond. Virtually all of the reciprocity-type hunters and gatherers were destroyed or forced into remote areas by bigger and more powerful societies that maximized production and population and that were organized by governing classes. At bottom, this replacement was essentially a matter of the ability of larger, denser, and better-organized societies to defeat simple hunters and gatherers in armed conflict. It was work hard or perish.

DISCUSSION QUESTIONS

1. What are the various functions of the potlatch, according to Marvin Harris?
2. How does Harris explain the fact that some groups (such as the Kwakuitl) encourage competitive feasting/gift-giving while others (such as the Eskimos) do not?
3. How do people in the United States compete for social status? Can you see any parallels with the potlatch?

RESOURCES ON THE INTERNET

InfoTrac College Edition

(http://infotrac.thomsonlearning.com/index.html)

You can find further relevant readings by searching *InfoTrac College Edition,* an online library with access to thousands of scholarly and popular periodicals. Below are suggested search terms for this article:

- potlatch
- redistribution
- social status

Anthropology Online: Wadsworth's Anthropology Resource Center

(http://anthropology.wadsworth.com)

The Wadsworth Anthropology Resource Center contains a wealth of information and useful tools for students including information on careers in anthropology.

6

When Brothers Share a Wife

MELVYN C. GOLDSTEIN

Anthropologists recognize three major types of marriage based on the number of spouses permitted: monogamy (the marriage of one woman to one man at a time); polygyny (the marriage of a man to more than one woman at a time); and polyandry (the marriage of a woman to two or more men at a time. The rarest of the three forms is polyandry, practiced in fewer than one percent of the cultures in the world. In this selection, Melvyn Goldstein explores fraternal polyandry (two or more brothers married to the same woman) as practiced among Tibetans. Whereas most Americans uncritically dismiss any form of plural marriage as inherently immoral, Goldstein reveals the basic rationale behind polyandry which, for Tibetans, make it a logical form of marriage. He argues that when brothers marry a single wife, they are able to preserve scarce resources by actually keeping their family land in tact.

Eager to reach home, Dorje drives his yaks hard over the 17,000-foot mountain pass, stopping only once to rest. He and his two older brothers, Pema and Sonam, are jointly marrying a woman from the next village in a few weeks, and he has to help with the preparations.

Dorje, Pema, and Sonam are Tibetans living in Limi, a 200-square-mile area in the northwest corner of Nepal, across the border from Tibet. The form of marriage they are about to enter—fraternal polyandry in anthropological parlance—is one of the world's rarest forms of marriage but is not uncommon in Tibetan society, where it has been practiced from time immemorial. For many Tibetan social strata, it traditionally represented the ideal form of marriage and family.

The mechanics of fraternal polyandry are simple. Two, three, four, or more brothers jointly take a wife, who leaves her home to come and live with them. Traditionally, marriage was arranged by parents, with children, particularly females, having little or no say. This is changing somewhat nowadays, but it is still unusual for children to marry without their parents' consent. Marriage ceremonies vary by income and region and range from all the brothers sitting together as grooms to only the eldest one formally doing so. The age of the brothers plays an important role in determining this: very young brothers almost never participate in actual marriage ceremonies, although they typically join the marriage when they reach their midteens.

The eldest brother is normally dominant in terms of authority, that is, in managing the household, but all the brothers share the work and participate as sexual partners. Tibetan males and females do not find the sexual aspect of sharing a spouse the least bit unusual, repulsive, or scandalous, and the norm is for the wife to treat all the brothers the same.

Offspring are treated similarly. There is no attempt to link children biologically to particular brothers, and a brother shows no favoritism toward his child even if he knows he is the real father because, for example, his other brothers were away at the time the wife became pregnant. The children, in turn, consider all of the brothers as their fathers and treat them equally, even if they also know who is their real father. In some regions children use the term "father" for the eldest brother and "father's brother" for the others, while in other areas they call all the brothers by one term, modifying this by the use of "elder" and "younger."

Unlike our own society, where monogamy is the only form of marriage permitted, Tibetan society allows a variety of marriage types, including monogamy, fraternal polyandry, and polygyny. Fraternal polyandry and monogamy are the most common forms of marriage, while polygyny typically occurs in cases where the first wife is barren. The widespread practice of fraternal polyandry, therefore, is not the outcome of a law requiring brothers to marry jointly. There is choice, and in fact, divorce traditionally was relatively simple in Tibetan society. If a brother in a polyandrous marriage became dissatisfied and wanted to separate, he simply left the main house and set up his own household. In such cases, all the children stayed in the main household with the remaining brother(s), even if the departing brother was known to be the real father of one or more of the children.

The Tibetans' own explanation for choosing fraternal polyandry is materialistic. For example, when I asked Dorje why he decided to marry with his two brothers rather than take him own wife, he thought for a moment, then said it prevented the division of his family's farm (and animals) and thus facilitated all of them achieving a higher standard of living. And when I later asked Dorje's bride whether it wasn't difficult for her to cope with three brothers as husbands, she laughed and echoed the rationale of avoiding fragmentation of the family and land, adding that she expected to be better off economically, since she would have three husbands working for her and her children.

Exotic as it may seem to Westerners, Tibetan fraternal polyandry is thus in many ways analogous to the way primogeniture functioned in nineteenth-century England. Primogeniture dictated that the eldest son inherited the family estate, while younger sons had to leave home and seek their own employment—for example, in the military or the clergy. Primogeniture maintained family estates intact over generations by permitting only one heir per generation. Fraternal polyandry also accomplishes this but does so by keeping all the brothers together with just one wife so that there is only one *set* of heirs per generation.

While Tibetans believe that in this way fraternal polyandry reduces the risk of family fission, monogamous marriages among brothers need not necessarily precipitate the division of the family estate: brothers could continue to live together, and the family land could continue to be worked jointly. When I asked Tibetans about this, however, they invariably responded that such joint families are unstable because each wife is primarily oriented to her own children and interested in their success and well-being over that of the children of the other wives. For example, if the youngest brother's wife had three sons while the eldest brother's wife had only one daughter, the wife of the youngest brother might begin to demand more resources for her children since, as males, they represent the future of the family. Thus, the children from different wives in the same generation are competing sets of heirs, and this makes such families inherently unstable. Tibetans perceive that conflict will spread from the wives to their husbands and consider this likely to cause family fission. Consequently, it is almost never done.

Although Tibetans see an economic advantage to fraternal polyandry, they do not value the sharing of a wife as an end in itself. On the contrary, they articulate a number of problems inherent in the practice. For example, because authority is customarily exercised by the eldest brother, his younger male siblings have to subordinate themselves with little hope of changing their status within the family. When these younger brothers are aggressive and individualistic, tensions and difficulties often occur despite there being only one set of heirs.

In addition, tension and conflict may arise in polyandrous families because of sexual favoritism. The bride normally sleeps with the eldest brother, and the two have the responsibility to see to it that the other males have opportunities for sexual access. Since the Tibetan subsistence economy requires males to travel a lot, the temporary absence of one or more brothers facilitates this, but there are also other rotation practices. The cultural ideal unambiguously calls for the wife to show equal affection and sexuality to each of the brothers (and vice versa), but deviations from this ideal occur, especially when there is a sizable difference in age between the partners in the marriage.

Dorje's family represents just such a potential situation. He is fifteen years old and his two older brothers are twenty-five and twenty-two years old. The new bride is twenty-three years old, eight years Dorje's senior. Sometimes such a bride finds the youngest husband immature and adolescent and does not treat him with equal affection; alternatively, she may find his youth attractive and lavish special attention on him. Apart from that consideration, when a younger male like Dorje grows up, he may consider his wife "ancient" and prefer the company of a woman his own age or younger. Consequently, although men and women do not find the idea of sharing a bride or a bridegroom repulsive, individual likes and dislikes can cause familial discord.

Two reasons have commonly been offered for the perpetuation of fraternal polyandry in Tibet: that Tibetans practice female infanticide and therefore have to marry polyandrously, owing to a shortage of females; and that Tibet, lying at extremely high altitudes, is so barren and bleak that Tibetans would starve without resort to this mechanism. A Jesuit who lived in Tibet during the eighteenth century articulated this second view: "One reason for this most odious custom is the sterility of the soil, and the small amount of land that can be cultivated owing to the lack of water. The crops may suffice if the brothers all live together, but if they form separate families they would be reduced to beggary."

Both explanations are wrong, however. Not only has there never been institutionalized female infanticide in Tibet, but Tibetan society gives females considerable rights, including inheriting the family estate in the absence of brothers. In such cases, the woman takes a bridegroom who comes to live in her family and adopts her family's name and identity. Moreover, there is no demographic evidence of a shortage of females. In Limi, for example, there were (in 1974) sixty females and fifty-three males in the fifteen- to thirty-five-year age category, and many adult females were unmarried.

The second reason is also incorrect. The climate in Tibet is extremely harsh, and ecological factors do play a major role perpetuating polyandry, but polyandry is not a means of preventing starvation. It is characteristic, not of the poorest segments of the society, but rather of the peasant landowning families.

In the old society, the landless poor could not realistically aspire to prosperity, but they did not fear starvation. There was a persistent labor shortage throughout Tibet, and very poor families with little or no land and few animals could subsist through agricultural labor, tenant farming, craft occupations such as carpentry, or by working as servants. Although the per person family income could increase somewhat if brothers married polyandrously and pooled their wages, in the absence of inheritable land, the advantage of fraternal polyandry was not generally sufficient to prevent them from setting up their own households. A more skilled or energetic younger brother could do as well or better alone, since he would completely control his income and would not have to share it with his siblings. Consequently, while there was and is some polyandry among the poor, it is much less frequent and more prone to result in divorce and family fission.

An alternative reason for the persistence of fraternal polyandry is that it reduces population growth (and thereby reduces the pressure on resources) by relegating some females to lifetime spinsterhood. Fraternal polyandrous marriages in Limi (in 1974) averaged 2.35 men per woman, and not surprisingly, 31 percent of the females of child-bearing age (twenty to forty-nine) were unmarried. These spinsters either continued to live at home, set up their own households, or worked as servants for other families. They could also become Buddhist nuns. Being unmarried is not synonymous with exclusion from the reproductive pool. Discreet extramarital relationships are tolerated, and actually half of the adult unmarried women in Limi had one or more children. They raised these children as single mothers, working for wages or weaving cloth and blankets for sale. As a group, however, the unmarried woman had far fewer offspring than the married women, averaging only 0.7 children per woman, compared with 3.3 for married women, whether polyandrous, monogamous, or polygynous. While polyandry helps regulate population, this function of polyandry is not consciously perceived by Tibetans and is not the reason they consistently choose it.

If neither a shortage of females nor the fear of starvation perpetuates fraternal polyandry, what motivates brothers, particularly younger brothers, to opt for this system of marriage? From the perspective of the younger brother in a landholding family, the main incentive is the attainment or maintenance of the good life. With polyandry, he can expect a more secure and higher standard of living, with access not only to this family's land and animals but also to its inherited collection of clothes, jewelry, rugs, saddles, and horses. In addition, he will experience less work pressure and much greater security because all responsibility does not fall on one "father." For Tibetan brothers, the question is whether to trade off the greater personal freedom inherent in monogamy for the real or potential economic security, affluence, and social prestige associated with life in a larger, labor-rich polyandrous family.

A brother thinking of separating from his polyandrous marriage and taking his own wife would face various disadvantages. Although in the majority of Tibetan regions all brothers theoretically have rights to their family's estate, in reality Tibetans are reluctant to divide their land into small fragments. Generally, a younger brother who insists on leaving the family will receive only a small plot of land, if that. Because of its power and wealth, the rest of the family usually can block any attempt of the younger brother to increase his share of land through litigation. Moreover, a younger brother may not even get a house and cannot expect to receive much above the minimum in terms of movable possessions, such as furniture, pots, and pans. Thus, a brother contemplating going it on his own must plan on achieving economic security and the good life not through inheritance but through his own work.

The obvious solution for younger brothers—creating new fields from virgin land—is generally not a feasible option. Most Tibetan populations live at high altitudes (above 12,000 feet), where arable land is extremely scarce. For example, in Dorje's village, agriculture ranges only from about 12,900 feet, the lowest point in the area, to 13,300 feet. Above that altitude, early frost and snow destroy the staple barley crop. Furthermore, because of the low rainfall caused by the Himalayan rain shadow, many areas in Tibet and northern Nepal that are within the appropriate altitude range for agriculture have no reliable sources of irrigation. In the end, although there is plenty of unused land in such areas, most of it is either too high or too arid.

Even where unused land capable of being farmed exists, clearing the land and building the substantial terraces necessary for irrigation constitute a great undertaking. Each plot has to be completely dug out to a depth of two to two and half feet so that the large rocks and boulders can be removed. At best, a man might be able to bring a few new fields under cultivation in the first years after separating from his brothers, but he could not expect to acquire substantial amounts of arable land this way.

In addition, because of the limited farmland, the Tibetan subsistence economy characteristically includes a strong emphasis on animal husbandry. Tibetan farmers regularly maintain cattle, yaks, goats, and sheep, grazing them in the areas too high for agriculture. These herds produce wool, milk, cheese, butter, meat, and skins. To obtain these resources, however, shepherds must accompany the animals on a daily basis. When first setting up a monogamous household, a younger brother like Dorje would find it difficult to both farm and manage animals.

In traditional Tibetan society, there was an even more critical factor that operated to perpetuate fraternal polyandry—a form of hereditary servitude somewhat analogous to serfdom in Europe. Peasants were tied to large estates held by aristocrats, monasteries, and the Lhasa government. They were allowed the use of some farmland to produce their own subsistence but were required to provide taxes in kind and corvée (free labor) to their lords. The corvée was a substantial hardship, since a peasant household was in many cases required to furnish the lord with one laborer daily for most of the year and more on specific occasions such as the harvest. This enforced labor, along with the lack of new land and ecological pressure to pursue both agriculture and animal husbandry, made polyandrous families particularly beneficial. The polyandrous family allowed an internal division of adult labor, maximizing economic advantage. For example, while the wife worked the family fields, one brother could perform the lord's corvée, another could look after the animals, and a third could engage in trade.

Although social scientists often discount other people's explanations of why they do things, in the case of Tibetan fraternal polyandry, such explanations are very close to the truth. The custom, however, is very sensitive to changes in its political and economic milieu and, not surprisingly, is in decline in most Tibetan areas. Made less important by the elimination of the traditional serf-based economy, it is disparaged by the dominant non-Tibetan leaders of India, China, and Nepal. New opportunities for economic and social mobility in these countries, such as the tourist trade and government employment, are also eroding the rationale for polyandry, and so it may vanish within the next generation.

DISCUSSION QUESTIONS

1. What is meant by primogeniture?
2. How can conflicts occur between brothers married to the same woman in a polyandrous system of marriage?
3. Why is the practice of polyandry becoming less frequent in Tibet?

RESOURCES ON THE INTERNET

InfoTrac College Edition

(http://infotrac.thomsonlearning.com/index.html)

You can find further relevant readings by searching *InfoTrac College Edition,* an online library with access to thousands of scholarly and popular periodicals. Following are suggested search terms for this article:

- polyandry
- monogamy
- family planning

Anthropology Online: Wadsworth's Anthropology Resource Center

(http://anthropology.wadsworth.com)

The Wadsworth Anthropology Resource Center contains a wealth of information and useful tools for students including information on careers in anthropology.

7

Death Without Weeping

NANCY SCHEPER-HUGHES

Most anthropologists acknowledge a special emotional bond that exists between mother and child, owing to the physical nature of pregnancy and birth, in whatever culture they may be found. But can these strong psychological bonds undergo significant changes in the face of severe economic and social conditions? In this article about mothers in a Brazilian shantytown, anthropologist Nancy Scheper-Hughes examines how extreme poverty, deprivation, hunger, and economic exploitation can cause mothers not to mourn the death of their children. She found that mothers living under these extreme conditions develop a strategy of delayed attachment to their children, withholding emotional involvement until they are reasonably sure the child will survive. Such a strategy—while appearing cruel and unfeeling to those of us in our comfortable, middle-class surroundings—is really an emotional coping strategy for mothers living with an extraordinarily high infant and child mortality rate. Rather than seeing "mother love" as an absolute cultural universal, Scheper-Hughes suggests that, under these extreme conditions, it is a luxury reserved for those children who survive. This article, and the book on which it is based written in 1992, provide a thoughtful and wrenching analysis of how poverty and injustice can lead to the demise of a mother's basic human right of weeping for her dead children.

Scheper-Hughes reminds us that cultures are not isolated, insulated entities which determine people's behavior. Instead we are compelled to look at the factors from the wider society—such as political, religious, and economic institutions—impinging on people's behavior.

I have seen death without weeping
The destiny of the Northeast is death
Cattle they kill
To the people they do something worse

—ANONYMOUS
BRAZILIAN SINGER (1965)

"Why do the church bells ring so often?" I asked Nailza de Arruda soon after I moved into a corner of her tiny mud-walled hut near the top of the shantytown called the Alto do Cruzeiro (Crucifix Hill). I was then a Peace Corps volunteer and a community development/health worker. It was the dry and blazing hot summer of 1965, the months following the military coup in Brazil, and save for the rusty, clanging bells of N. S. das

From *Natural History,* October 1989, pp. 8, 10, 12, 14, 16.

Dores Church, an eerie quiet had settled over the market town that I call Bom Jesus da Mata. Beneath the quiet, however, there was chaos and panic. "It's nothing," replied Nailza, "just another little angel gone to heaven."

Nailza had sent more than her share of little angels to heaven, and sometimes at night I could hear her engaged in a muffled but passionate discourse with one of them, two-year-old Joana. Joana's photograph, taken as she lay propped up in her tiny cardboard coffin, her eyes open, hung on a wall next to one of Nailza and Ze Antonio taken on the day they eloped.

Nailza could barely remember the other infants and babies who came and went in close succession. Most had died unnamed and were hastily baptized in their coffins. Few lived more than a month or two. Only Joana, properly baptized in church at the close of her first year and placed under the protection of a powerful saint, Joan of Arc, had been expected to live. And Nailza had dangerously allowed herself to love the little girl.

In addressing the dead child, Nailza's voice would range from tearful imploring to angry recrimination: "Why did you leave me? Was your patron saint so greedy that she could not allow me one child on this earth?" Ze Antonio advised me to ignore Nailza's odd behavior, which he understood as a kind of madness that, like the birth and death of children, came and went. Indeed, the premature birth of a stillborn son some months later "cured" Nailza of her "inappropriate" grief, and the day came when she removed Joana's photo and carefully packed it away.

More than fifteen years elapsed before I returned to the Alto do Cruzeiro, and it was anthropology that provided the vehicle of my return. Since 1982 I have returned several times in order to pursue a problem that first attracted my attention in the 1960s. My involvement with the people of the Alto do Cruzeiro now spans a quarter of a century and three generations of parenting in a community where mothers and daughters are often simultaneously pregnant.

The Alto do Cruzeiro is one of three shantytowns surrounding the large market town of Bom Jesus in the sugar plantation zone of Pernambuco in Northeast Brazil, one of the many zones of neglect that have emerged in the shadow of the now tarnished economic miracle of Brazil. For the women and children of the Alto do Cruzeiro the only miracle is that some of them have managed to stay alive at all.

The Northeast is a region of vast proportions (approximately twice the size of Texas) and of equally vast social and developmental problems. The nine states that make up the region are the poorest in the country and are representative of the Third World within a dynamic and rapidly industrializing nation. Despite waves of migrations from the interior to the teeming shantytowns of coastal cities, the majority still live in rural areas on farms and ranches, sugar plantations and mills.

Life expectancy in the Northeast is only forty years, largely because of the appallingly high rate of infant and child mortality. Approximately one million children in Brazil under the age of five die each year. The children of the Northeast, especially those born in shantytowns on the periphery of urban life, are at a very high risk of death. In these areas, children are born without the traditional protection of breast-feeding, subsistence gardens, stable marriages, and multiple adult caretakers that exists in the interior. In the hillside shantytowns that spring up around cities or, in this case, interior market towns, marriages are brittle, single parenting is the norm, and women are frequently forced into the shadow economy of domestic work in the homes of the rich or into unprotected and oftentimes "scab" wage labor on the surrounding sugar plantations, where they clear land for planting and weed for a pittance, sometimes less than a dollar a day. The women of the Alto may not bring their babies with them into the homes of the wealthy, where the often-sick infants are considered sources of contamination, and they cannot carry the little ones to the riverbanks where they wash clothes because the river is heavily infested with schistosomes and other deadly parasites. Nor can they carry their young children to the plantations, which are often several miles away. At wages of a dollar a day, the women of the Alto cannot hire baby sitters. Older children who are not in school will sometimes serve as somewhat indifferent caretakers. But any child not in school is also expected to find wage work. In most cases, babies are simply left at home alone, the door securely fastened. And so many also die alone and unattended.

Bom Jesus da Mata, centrally located in the plantation zone of Pernambuco, is within commuting distance of several sugar plantations and mills. Consequently, Bom Jesus has been a magnet for rural workers forced off their small subsistence plots by large landowners wanting to use every available piece of land for sugar cultivation. Initially, the rural migrants to Bom Jesus were squatters who were given tacit approval by the mayor to put up temporary straw huts on each of the three hills overlooking the town. The Alto do Cruzeiro is the oldest, the largest, and the poorest of the shantytowns. Over the past three decades many of the original migrants have become permanent residents, and the primitive and temporary straw huts have been replaced by small homes (usually of two rooms) made of wattle and daub, sometimes covered with plaster. The more affluent residents use bricks and tiles. In most Alto homes, dangerous kerosene lamps have been replaced by light bulbs. The once tattered rural garb, often fashioned from used sugar sacking, has likewise been replaced by store-bought clothes, often castoffs from a wealthy *patrão* (boss). The trappings are modern, but the hunger, sickness, and death that they conceal are traditional, deeply rooted in a history of feudalism, exploitation, and institutionalized dependency.

My research agenda never wavered. The questions I addressed first crystallized during a veritable "die-off" of Alto babies during a severe drought in 1965. The food and water shortages and the political and economic chaos occasioned by the military coup were reflected in the handwritten entries of births and deaths in the dusty, yellowed pages of the ledger books kept at the public registry office in Bom Jesus. More than 350 babies died in the Alto during 1965 alone—this from a shantytown population of little more than 5,000. But that wasn't what surprised me. There were reasons enough for the deaths in the miserable conditions of shantytown life. What puzzled me was the seeming indifference of Alto women to the death of their infants, and their willingness to attribute to their own tiny offspring an aversion to life that made their death seem wholly natural, indeed all but anticipated.

Although I found that it was possible, and hardly difficult, to rescue infants and toddlers from death by diarrhea and dehydration with a simple sugar, salt, and water solution (even bottled Coca-Cola worked fine), it was more difficult to enlist a mother herself in the rescue of a child she perceived as ill-fated for life or better off dead, or to convince her to take back into her threatened and besieged home a baby she had already come to think of as an angel rather than as a son or daughter.

I learned that the high expectancy of death, and the ability to face child death with stoicism and equanimity, produced patterns of nurturing that differentiated between those infants thought of as thrivers and survivors and those thought of as born already "wanting to die." The survivors were nurtured, while stigmatized, doomed infants were left to die, as mothers say, *a mingua,* "of neglect." Mothers stepped back and allowed nature to take its course. This pattern, which I call mortal selective neglect, is called passive infanticide by anthropologist Marvin Harris. The Alto situation, although culturally specific in the form that it takes, is not unique to Third World shantytown communities and may have its correlates in our own impoverished urban communities in some cases of "failure to thrive" infants.

I use as an example the story of Zezinho, the thirteen-month-old toddler of one of my neighbors, Lourdes. I became involved with Zezinho when I was called in to help Lourdes in the delivery of another child, this one a fair and robust little tyke with a lusty cry. I noted that while Lourdes showed great interest in the newborn, she totally ignored Zezinho who, wasted and severely malnourished, was curled up in a fetal position on a piece of urine- and feces-soaked cardboard placed under his mother's hammock. Eyes open and vacant, mouth slack, the little boy seemed doomed.

When I carried Zezinho up to the community day-care center at the top of the hill, the Alto women who took turns caring for one another's children (in order to free themselves for part-time work in the cane fields or washing clothes) laughed at my efforts to save Ze, agreeing with Lourdes that here was a baby without a ghost of a chance. Leave him alone, they cautioned. It makes no sense to fight with death. But I did do battle with Ze, and after several weeks of force-feeding (malnourished babies lose their interest in food), Ze began to succumb to my ministrations. He acquired some flesh across his taut chest bones, learned to sit up, and even tried to smile. When he seemed well enough, I returned him to Lourdes in her miserable scrap-material lean-to, but not without guilt about what I had done. I wondered whether returning Ze was at all fair to Lourdes and to his little brother. But I was busy and washed my hands of the matter. And Lourdes did seem more interested in Ze now that he was looking more human.

When I returned in 1982, there was Lourdes among the women who formed my sample of Alto mothers—still struggling to put together some semblance of life for a now grown Ze and her five other surviving children. Much was made of my reunion with Ze in 1982, and everyone enjoyed retelling the story of Ze's rescue and of how his mother had given him up for dead. Ze would laugh the loudest when told how I had had to force-feed him like a fiesta turkey. There was no hint of guilt on the part of Lourdes and no resentment on the part of Ze. In fact, when questioned in private as to who was the best friend he ever had in life, Ze took a long drag on his cigarette and answered without a trace of irony, "Why my mother, of course." "But of course," I replied.

Part of learning how to mother in the Alto do Cruzeiro is learning when to let go of a child who shows that it "wants" to die or that it has no "knack" or no "taste" for life. Another part is learning when it is safe to let oneself love a child. Frequent child death remains a powerful shaper of maternal thinking and practice. In the absence of firm expectation that a child will survive, mother love as we conceptualize it (whether in popular terms or in the psychobiological notion of maternal bonding) is attenuated and delayed with consequences for infant survival. In an environment already precarious to young life, the emotional detachment of mothers toward some of their babies contributes even further to the spiral of high mortality—high fertility in a kind of macabre lock-step dance of death.

The average woman of the Alto experiences 9.5 pregnancies, 3.5 child deaths, and 1.5 stillbirths. Seventy percent of all child deaths in the Alto occur in the first six months of life, and 82 percent by the end of the first year. Of all deaths in the community each year, about 45 percent are of children under the age of five.

Women of the Alto distinguish between child deaths understood as natural (caused by diarrhea and communicable diseases) and those resulting from sorcery, the evil eye, or other magical or supernatural afflictions. They also recognize a large category of infant deaths seen as fated and inevitable. These hopeless cases are classified by mothers under the folk terminology "child sickness" or "child attack." Women say that there are at least fourteen different types of hopeless child sickness, but most can be subsumed under two categories—chronic and acute. The chronic cases refer to infants who are born small and wasted. They are deathly pale, mothers say, as well as weak and passive. They demonstrate no vital force, no liveliness. They do not suck vigorously; they hardly cry. Such babies can be this way at birth or they can be born sound but soon show no resistance, no "fight" against the common crises of infancy: diarrhea, respiratory infections, tropical fevers.

The acute cases are those doomed infants who die suddenly and violently. They are taken by stealth overnight, often following convulsions that bring on head banging, shaking, grimacing, and shrieking. Women say it is horrible to look at such a baby. If the infant begins to foam at the mouth or gnash its teeth or go rigid with its eyes turned back inside its head, there is absolutely no hope. The infant is "put aside"—left alone—often on the floor in a back room, and allowed to die. These symptoms (which accompany high fevers, dehydration, third-stage malnutrition, and encephalitis) are equated by Alto women with madness, epilepsy, and worst of all, rabies, which is greatly feared and highly stigmatized.

Most of the infants presented to me as suffering from chronic child sickness were tiny, wasted famine victims, while those labeled as victims of acute child attack seemed to be infants suffering from the deliriums of high fever or the convulsions that can accompany electrolyte imbalance in dehydrated babies.

Local midwives and traditional healers, praying women, as they are called, advise Alto women on when to allow a baby to die. One midwife explained: "If I can see that a baby was born unfortuitously, I tell the mother that she need not wash the infant or give it a cleansing tea. I tell her just to dust the infant with baby powder and wait for it to die." Allowing nature to take its course is not seen as sinful by these often very devout Catholic women. Rather, it is understood as cooperating with God's plan.

Often I have been asked how consciously women of the Alto behave in this regard. I would have to say that consciousness is always shifting between allowed and disallowed levels of awareness. For example, I was awakened early one morning in 1987 by two neighborhood children who had been sent to fetch me to a hastily organized wake for a two-month-old infant whose mother I had unsuccessfully urged to breast-feed. The infant was being sustained on sugar water, which the mother referred to as *soro* (serum), using a medical term for the infant's starvation regime in light of his chronic diarrhea. I had cautioned the mother that an infant could not live on *soro* forever.

The two girls urged me to console the young mother by telling her that it was "too bad" that her infant was so weak that Jesus had to take him. They were coaching me in proper Alto etiquette. I agreed, of course, but asked, "And what do *you* think?" Xoxa, the eleven-year-old, looked down at her dusty flip-flops and blurted out, "Oh, Dona Nanci, that baby never got enough to eat, but you must never say that!" And so the death of hungry babies remains one of the best kept secrets of life in Bom Jesus da Mata.

Most victims are waked quickly and with a minimum of ceremony. No tears are shed, and the neighborhood children form a tiny procession, carrying the baby to the town graveyard where it will join a multitude of others. Although a few fresh flowers may be scattered over the tiny grave, no stone or wooden cross will mark the place, and the same spot will be reused within a few months' time. The mother will never visit the grave, which soon becomes an anonymous one.

What, then, can be said of these women? What emotions, what sentiments motivate them? How are they able to do what, in fact, must be done? What does mother love mean in this inhospitable context? Are grief, mourning, and melancholia present, although deeply repressed? If so, where shall we look for them? And if not, how are we to understand the moral visions and moral sensibilities that guide their actions?

I have been criticized more than once for presenting an unflattering portrait of poor Brazilian women, women who are, after all, themselves the victims of severe social and institutional neglect. I have described these women as allowing some of their children to die, as if this were an unnatural and inhuman act rather than, as I would assert, the way any one of us might act, reasonably and rationally, under similarly desperate conditions. Perhaps I have not emphasized enough the real pathogens in this environment of high risk: poverty, deprivation, sexism, chronic hunger, and economic exploitation. If mother love is, as many psychologists and some feminists believe, a seemingly natural and universal maternal script, what does it mean to women for whom scarcity, loss, sickness, and deprivation have made that love frantic and robbed them of their grief, seeming to turn their hearts to stone?

Throughout much of human history—as in a great deal of the impoverished Third World today—women have had to give birth and to nurture children under ecological conditions and social arrangements hostile to child survival, as well as to their own well-being. Under circumstances of high childhood mortality, patterns of selective neglect and passive infanticide may be seen as active survival strategies.

They also seem to be fairly common practices historically and across cultures. In societies characterized by high childhood mortality and by a correspondingly high (replacement) fertility, cultural practices of infant and child care tend to be organized primarily around survival goals. But what this means is a pragmatic recognition that not all of one's children can be expected to live. The nervousness about child survival in areas of northeast Brazil, northern India, or Bangladesh, where a 30 percent or 40 percent mortality rate in the first years of life is common, can lead to forms of delayed attachment and a casual or benign neglect that serves to weed out the worst bets so as to enhance the life chances of healthier siblings, including those yet to be born. Practices similar to those that I am describing have been recorded for parts of Africa, India, and Central America.

Life in the Alto do Cruzeiro resembles nothing so much as a battlefield or an emergency room in an overcrowded inner-city public hospital. Consequently, morality is guided by a kind of "lifeboat ethics," the morality of triage. The seemingly studied indifference toward the suffering of some of their infants, conveyed in such sayings as "little critters have no feelings," is understandable in light of these women's obligation to carry on with their reproductive and nurturing lives.

In their slowness to anthropomorphize and personalize their infants, everything is mobilized so as to prevent maternal overattachment and, therefore, grief at death. The bereaved mother is told not to cry, that her tears will dampen the wings of her little angel so that she cannot fly up to her heavenly home. Grief at the death of an angel is not only inappropriate, it is a symptom of madness and of a profound lack of faith.

Infant death becomes routine in an environment in which death is anticipated and bets are hedged. While the routinization of death in the context of shantytown life is not hard to understand, and quite possible to empathize with, its routinization in the formal institutions of public life in Bom Jesus is not as easy to accept uncritically. Here the social production of indifference takes on a different, even a malevolent, cast.

In a society where triplicates of every form are required for the most banal events (registering a car, for example), the registration of infant and child death is informal, incomplete, and rapid. It requires no documentation, takes less than five minutes, and demands no witnesses other than office clerks. No questions are asked concerning the circumstances of the death, and the cause of death is left blank, unquestioned and unexamined. A neighbor, grandmother, older sibling, or common-law husband may register the death. Since most infants die at home, there is no question of a medical record.

From the registry office, the parent proceeds to the town hall, where the mayor will give him or her a voucher for a free baby coffin. The full-time municipal coffinmaker cannot tell you exactly how many baby coffins are dispatched each week. It varies, he says, with the seasons. There are more needed during the drought months and during the big festivals of Carnaval and Christmas and São Joao's Day because people are too busy, he supposes, to take their babies to the clinic. Record keeping is sloppy.

Similarly, there is a failure on the part of city-employed doctors working at two free clinics to recognize the malnutrition of babies who are weighed, measured, and immunized without comment and as if they were not, in fact, anemic, stunted, fussy, and irritated starvation babies. At best the mothers are told to pick up free vitamins or a health "tonic" at the municipal chambers. At worst, clinic personnel will give tranquilizers and sleeping pills to quiet the hungry cries of "sick-to-death" Alto babies.

The church, too, contributes to the routinization of, and indifference toward, child death. Traditionally, the local Catholic church taught patience and resignation to domestic tragedies that were said to reveal the imponderable workings of God's will. If an infant died suddenly, it was because a particular saint had claimed the child. The infant would be an angel in the service of his or her heavenly patron. It would be wrong, a sign of a lack of faith, to weep for a child with such good fortune. The infant funeral was, in the past, an event celebrated with joy. Today, however, under the new regime of "liberation theology," the bells of N.S. das Dores parish church no longer peal for the death of Alto babies, and no priest accompanies the procession of angels to the cemetery where their bodies are disposed of casually and without ceremony. Children bury children in Bom Jesus da Mata. In this most Catholic of communities, the coffin is handed to the disabled and irritable municipal gravedigger, who often chides the children for one reason or another. It may be that the coffin is larger than expected and the gravedigger can find no appropriate space. The children do not wait for the gravedigger to complete his task. No prayers are recited and no sign of the cross made as the tiny coffin goes into its shallow grave.

When I asked the local priest, Padre Marcos, about the lack of church ceremony surrounding infant and childhood death today in Bom Jesus, he replied: "In the old days, child death was richly celebrated. But those were the baroque customs of a conservative church that wallowed in death and misery. The new church is a church of hope and joy. We no longer celebrate the death of child angels. We try to tell mothers that Jesus doesn't want all the dead babies they send him." Similarly, the new church has changed its baptismal customs, now often refusing to baptize dying babies brought to the back door of a church or rectory. The mothers are scolded by the church attendants and told to go home and take care of their sick babies. Baptism, they are told, is for the living; it is not to be confused with the sacrament of extreme unction, which is the anointing of the dying. And so it appears to the women of the Alto that even the church has turned away from them, denying the traditional comfort of folk Catholicism.

The contemporary Catholic church is caught in the clutches of a double bind. The new theology of liberation imagines a kingdom of God on earth based on justice and equality, a world without hunger, sickness, or childhood mortality. At the same time, the church has not changed its official position on sexuality and reproduction, including its sanctions against birth control, abortion, and sterilization. The padre of Bom Jesus da Mata recognizes this contradiction intuitively, although he shies away from discussions on the topic, saying that he prefers to leave questions of family planning to the discretion and the "good consciences" of his impoverished parishioners. But this, of course, sidesteps the extent to which those good consciences have been shaped by traditional church teachings in Bom Jesus, especially by his recent predecessors. Hence, we can begin to see that the seeming indifference of Alto mothers toward the death of some of their infants is but a pale reflection of the official indifference of church and state to the plight of poor women and children.

Nonetheless, the women of Bom Jesus are survivors. One woman, Biu, told me her life history, returning again and again to the themes of child death, her first husband's suicide, abandonment by her father and later by her second husband, and all the other losses and disappointments she has suffered in her long forty-five years. She concluded with great force, reflecting on the days of Carnaval '88 that were fast approaching:

> No, Dona Nanci, I won't cry, and I won't waste my life thinking about it from morning to night. . . . Can I argue with God for the

state that I'm in? No! And so I'll dance and I'll jump and I'll play Carnaval! And yes, I'll laugh and people will wonder at a *pobre* like me who can have such a good time.

And no one did blame Biu for dancing in the streets during the four days of Carnaval—not even on Ash Wednesday, the day following Carnaval '88 when we all assembled hurriedly to assist in the burial of Mercea, Biu's beloved *casula,* her last-born daughter who had died at home of pneumonia during the festivities. The rest of the family barely had time to change out of their costumes. Severino, the child's uncle and godfather, sprinkled holy water over the little angel while he prayed: "Mercea, I don't know whether you were called, taken, or thrown out of this world. But look down at us from your heavenly home with tenderness, with pity, and with mercy." So be it.

DISCUSSION QUESTIONS

1. Why don't women in Bom Jesus, Brazil, grieve outwardly for their dead children?
2. Do you think that mother love is an innate human emotion? How do you think Scheper-Hughes would answer that question?
3. Are there any possible sociocultural changes in the overall social structure of Bom Jesus, Brazil, that might be made to change the way mothers deal with the death of their children?

(http://infotrac.thomsonlearning.com/index.html)

You can find further relevant readings by searching *InfoTrac College Edition,* an online library with access to thousands of scholarly and popular periodicals. Below are suggested search terms for this article:

- infant mortality rate
- maternal love

Anthropology Online: Wadsworth's Anthropology Resource Center

(http://anthropology.wadsworth.com)

The Wadsworth Anthropology Resource Center contains a wealth of information and useful tools for students including information on careers in anthropology.

8

Society and Sex Roles

ERNESTINE FRIEDL

Although it is possible to find societies in which gender inequalities are kept to a minimum, the overwhelming ethnographic and archaeological evidence suggests that females are subordinate to men in terms of exerting economic and political control. This gender asymmetry is so pervasive that some anthropologists over the years have concluded that this gender inequality is the result of biological differences between men and women. That is, men are dominant because of their greater size, physical strength, and innate aggressiveness. In this selection, Ernestine Friedl argues that the answer to this near universal male dominance lies more with economics than with biological predisposition.

A former president of the American Anthropological Association, Friedl argues that men tend to be dominant because they control the distribution of scarce resources in the society, both within and outside of the family. Quite apart from who produces the goods, "the person controlling the distribution of the limited and valued resources possesses the currency needed to create the obligations and alliances that are at the center of all political relations." Using ethnographic examples from foraging societies, Friedl shows how women have relative equality in those societies where they exercise some control over resources. Conversely, men are nearly totally dominant in those societies in which women have no control over scarce resources.

"Women must respond quickly to the demands of their husbands," says anthropologist Napoleon Chagnon describing the horticultural Yanomamo Indians of Venezuela. When a man returns from a hunting trip, "the woman, no matter what she is doing, hurries home and quietly but rapidly prepares a meal for her husband. Should the wife be slow in doing this, the husband is within his rights to beat her. Most reprimands . . . take the form of blows with the hand or with a piece of firewood. . . . Some of them chop their wives with the sharp edge of a machete or axe, or shoot them with a barbed arrow in some nonvital area, such as the buttocks or leg."

Among the Semai agriculturalists of central Malaya, when one person refuses the request of another, the offended party suffers *punan,* a mix-

From "Society and Sex Roles" by Ernestine Friedl in *Human Nature,* April 1978, pp. 68–75. Reprinted with permission from the author.

ture of emotional pain and frustration. "Enduring *punan* is commonest when a girl has refused the victim her sexual favors," reports Robert Dentan. "The jilted man's 'heart becomes sad.' He loses his energy and his appetite. Much of the time he sleeps, dreaming of his lost love. In this state he is in fact very likely to injure himself 'accidentally.'" The Semai are afraid of violence; a man would never strike a woman.

The social relationship between men and women has emerged as one of the principal disputes occupying the attention of scholars and the public in recent years. Although the discord is sharpest in the United States, the controversy has spread throughout the world. Numerous national and international conferences, including one in Mexico sponsored by the United Nations, have drawn together delegates from all walks of life to discuss such questions as the social and political rights of each sex, and even the basic nature of males and females.

Whatever their position, partisans often invoke examples from other cultures to support their ideas about the proper role of each sex. Because women are clearly subservient to men in many societies, like the Yanomamo, some experts conclude that the natural pattern is for men to dominate. But among the Semai no one has the right to command others, and in West Africa women are often chiefs. The place of women in these societies supports the argument of those who believe that sex roles are not fixed, that if there is a natural order, it allows for many different arrangements.

The argument will never be settled as long as the opposing sides toss examples from the world's cultures at each other like intellectual stones. But the effect of biological differences on male and female behavior can be clarified by looking at known examples of the earliest forms of human society and examining the relationship between technology, social organization, environment, and sex roles. The problem is to determine the conditions in which different degrees of male dominance are found, to try to discover the social and cultural arrangements that give rise to equality or inequality between the sexes, and to attempt to apply this knowledge to our understanding of the changes taking place in modern industrial society.

As Western history and the anthropological record have told us, equality between the sexes is rare; in most known societies females are subordinate. Male dominance is so widespread that it is virtually a human universal; societies in which women are consistently dominant do not exist and have never existed.

Evidence of a society in which women control all strategic resources like food and water, and in which women's activities are the most prestigious has never been found. The Iroquois of North America and the Lovedu of Africa came closest. Among the Iroquois, women raised food, controlled its distribution, and helped to choose male political leaders. Lovedu women ruled as queens, exchanged valuable cattle, led ceremonies, and controlled their own sex lives. But among both the Iroquois and the Lovedu, men owned the land and held other positions of power and prestige. Women were equal to men; they did not have ultimate authority over them. Neither culture was a true matriarchy.

Patriarchies are prevalent, and they appear to be strongest in societies in which men control significant goods that are exchanged with people outside the family. Regardless of who produces food, the person who gives it to others creates the obligations and alliances that are at the center of all political relations. The greater the male monopoly on the distribution of scarce items, the stronger their control of women seems to be. This is most obvious in relatively simple hunter-gatherer societies.

Hunter-gatherers, or foragers, subsist on wild plants, small land animals, and small river or sea creatures gathered by hand; large land animals and sea mammals hunted with spears, bows and arrows, and blow guns; and fish caught with hooks and nets. The 300,000 hunter-gatherers alive in the world today include the Eskimos, the Australian aborigines, and the Pygmies of Central Africa.

Foraging has endured for two million years and was replaced by farming and animal husbandry only 10,000 years ago; it covers more than 99 percent of human history. Our foraging ancestry is not far behind us and provides a clue to our understanding of the human condition.

Hunter-gatherers are people whose ways of life are technologically simple and socially and politically egalitarian. They live in small groups of 50 to 200 and have neither kings, nor priests, nor social classes. These conditions permit anthropologists to observe the essential bases for inequalities between the sexes without the distortions induced by the complexities of contemporary industrial society.

The source of male power among hunter-gatherers lies in their control of a scarce, hard to acquire, but necessary nutrient—animal protein. When men in a hunter-gatherer society return to camp with game, they divide the meat in some customary way. Among the !Kung San of Africa, certain parts of the animal are given to the owner of the arrow that killed the beast, to the first hunter to sight the game, to the one who threw the first spear, and to all men in the hunting party. After the meat has been divided, each hunter distributes his share to his blood relatives and his in-laws, who in turn share it with others. If an animal is large enough, every member of the band will receive some meat.

Vegetable foods, in contrast, are not distributed beyond the immediate household. Women give food to their children, to their husbands, to other members of the household, and rarely, to the occasional visitor. No one outside the family regularly eats any of the wild fruits and vegetables that are gathered by the women.

The meat distributed by the men is a public gift. Its source is widely known, and the donor expects a reciprocal gift when other men return from a successful hunt. He gains honor as a supplier of a scarce item and simultaneously obligates others to him.

These obligations constitute a form of power or control over others, both men and women. The opinions of hunters play an important part in decisions to move the village; good hunters attract the most desirable women; people in other groups join camps with good hunters; and hunters, because they already participate in an internal system of exchange, control exchange with other groups for flint, salt, and steel axes. The male monopoly on hunting unites men in a system of exchange and gives them power; gathering vegetable food does not give women equal power even among foragers who live in the tropics, where the food collected by women provides more than half the hunter-gatherer diet.

If dominance arises from a monopoly on big-game hunting, why has the male monopoly remained unchallenged? Some women are strong enough to participate in the hunt and their endurance is certainly equal to that of men. Dobe San women of the Kalahari Desert in Africa walk an average of 10 miles a day carrying from 15 to 33 pounds of food plus a baby.

Women do not hunt, I believe, because of four interrelated factors: variability in the supply of game; the different skills required for hunting and gathering; the incompatibility between carrying burdens and hunting; and the small size of seminomadic foraging populations.

Because the meat supply is unstable, foragers must make frequent expeditions to provide the band with gathered food. Environmental factors such as seasonal and annual variation in rainful often affect the size of the wildlife population. Hunters cannot always find game, and when they do encounter animals, they are not always successful in killing their prey. In northern latitudes, where meat is the primary food, periods of starvation are known in every generation. The irregularity of the game supply leads hunter-gatherers in areas where plant foods are available to depend on these predictable foods a good part of the time. Someone must gather the fruits, nuts, and roots and carry them back to camp to feed unsuccessful hunters, children, the elderly, and anyone who might not have gone foraging that day.

Foraging falls to the women because hunting and gathering cannot be combined on the same expedition. Although gatherers sometimes notice signs of game as they work, the skills required to track game are not the same as those required to find edible roots or plants. Hunters scan the horizon and the land for traces of large game; gatherers keep their eyes to the ground, studying the distribution of plants and the texture of the soil for hidden roots and animal holes. Even if a woman who was collecting plants came across the track of an antelope, she could not follow it; it is impossible to carry a load and hunt at the same time. Running with a heavy load is difficult, and should the animal be sighted, the hunter would be off balance and could neither shoot an arrow nor throw a spear accurately.

Pregnancy and child care would also present difficulties for a hunter. An unborn child affects a woman's body balance, as does a child in her arms, on her back, or slung at her side. Until they are two years old, many hunter-gatherer children are carried at all times, and until they are four, they are carried some of the time.

An observer might wonder why young women do not hunt until they become pregnant, or why mature women and men do not hunt and gather on alternate days, with some women staying in camp to act as wet nurses for the young. Apart from the effects hunting might have on a mother's milk production, there are two reasons. First, young girls begin to bear children as soon as they are physically mature and strong enough to hunt, and second, hunter-gatherer bands are so small that there are unlikely to be enough lactating women to serve as wet nurses. No hunter-gatherer group could afford to maintain a specialized female hunting force.

Because game is not always available, because hunting and gathering are specialized skills, because women carrying heavy loads cannot hunt, and because women in hunter-gatherer societies are usually either pregnant or caring for young children, for most of the last two million years of human history men have hunted and women have gathered.

If male dominance depends on controlling the supply of meat, then the degree of male dominance in a society should vary with the amount of meat available and the amount supplied by the men. Some regions, like the East African grasslands and the North American woodlands, abounded with species of large mammals; other zones, like tropical forests and semideserts, are thinly populated with prey. Many elements affect the supply of game, but theoretically, the less meat provided exclusively by the men, the more egalitarian the society.

All known hunter-gatherer societies fit into four basic types: those in which men and women work together in communal hunts and as teams gathering edible plants, as did the Washo Indians of North America; those in which men and women each collect their own plant foods although the men supply some meat to the group, as do the Hadza of Tanzania; those in which male hunters and female gatherers work apart but return to camp each evening to share their acquisitions, as do the Tiwi of North Australia; and those in which the men provide all the food by hunting large game, as do the Eskimo. In each case the extent of male dominance increases directly with the proportion of meat supplied by individual men and small hunting parties.

Among the most egalitarian of hunter-gatherer societies are the Washo Indians, who inhabited the valleys of the Sierra Nevada in what is now southern California and Nevada. In the spring they moved north to Lake Tahoe for the large fish runs of sucker and native trout. Everyone—men, women, and children—participated in the fishing. Women spent the summer gathering edible berries and seeds while the men continued to fish. In the fall some men hunted deer but the most important source of animal protein was the jack rabbit, which was captured in communal hunts. Men and women together drove the rabbits into nets tied end to end. To provide food for the winter, husbands and wives worked as teams in the late fall to collect pine nuts.

Since everyone participated in most food-gathering activities, there were no individual distributors of food and relatively little difference in male and female rights. Men and women were not segregated from each other in daily activities;

both were free to take lovers after marriage; both had the right to separate whenever they chose; menstruating women were not isolated from the rest of the group; and one of the two major Washo rituals celebrated hunting while the other celebrated gathering. Men were accorded more prestige if they had killed a deer, and men directed decisions about the seasonal movement of the group. But if no male leader stepped forward, women were permitted to lead. The distinctive feature of groups such as the Washo is the relative equality of the sexes.

The sexes are also relatively equal among the Hadza of Tanzania but this near-equality arises because men and women tend to work alone to feed themselves. They exchange little food. The Hadza lead a leisurely life in the seemingly barren environment of the East African Rift Gorge that is, in fact, rich in edible berries, roots, and small game. As a result of this abundance, from the time they are 10 years old, Hadza men and women gather much of their own food. Women take their young children with them into the bush, eating as they forage, and collect only enough food for a light family meal in the evening. The men eat berries and roots as they hunt for small game, and should they bring down a rabbit or a hyrax, they eat the meat on the spot. Meat is carried back to the camp and shared with the rest of the group only on those rare occasions when a poisoned arrow brings down a large animal—an impala, a zebra, an eland, or a giraffe.

Because Hadza men distribute little meat, their status is only slightly higher than that of the women. People flock to the camp of a good hunter and the camp might take on his name because of his popularity, but he is in no sense a leader of the group. A Hadza man and a woman have an equal right to divorce and each can repudiate a marriage simply by living apart for a few weeks. Couples tend to live in the same camp as the wife's mother but they sometimes make long visits to the camp of the husband's mother. Although a man may take more than one wife, most Hadza males cannot afford to indulge in this luxury. In order to maintain a marriage, a man must supply both his wife and his mother-in-law with some meat and trade goods, such as beads and cloth, and the Hadza economy gives few men the wealth to provide for more than one wife and mother-in-law. Washo equality is based on cooperation; Hadza equality is based on independence.

In contrast to both these groups, among the Tiwi of Melville and Bathurst Islands off the northern coast of Australia, male hunters dominate female gatherers. The Tiwi are representative of the most common form of foraging society, in which the men supply large quantities of meat, although less than half the food consumed by the group. Each morning Tiwi women, most with babies on their backs, scatter in different directions in search of vegetables, grubs, worms, and small game such as bandicoots, lizards, and opossums. To track the game, they use hunting dogs. On most days women return to camp with some meat and with baskets full of *korka,* the nut of a native palm, which is soaked and mashed to make a porridge-like dish. The Tiwi men do not hunt small game and do not hunt every day, but when they do they often return with kangaroo, large lizards, fish, and game birds.

The porridge is cooked separately by each household and rarely shared outside the family, but the meat is prepared by a volunteer cook, who can be male or female. After the cook takes one of the parts of the animal traditionally reserved for him or her, the animal's "boss," the one who caught it, distributes the rest to all near kin and then to all others residing with the band. Although the small game supplied by the women is distributed in the same way as the big game supplied by the men, Tiwi men are dominant because the game they kill provides most of the meat.

The power of Tiwi men is clearest in their betrothal practices. Among the Tiwi, a woman must always be married. To ensure this, female infants are betrothed at birth and widows are remarried at the gravesides of their late husbands. Men form alliances by exchanging daughters, sisters, and mothers in marriage and some collect as many as 25 wives. Tiwi men value the quantity and quality of the food many wives can collect and the many children they can produce.

The dominance of the men is offset somewhat by the influence of adult women in selecting their next husbands. Many women are active strategists in the political careers of their male relatives, but to the exasperation of some sons attempting to promote their own futures, widowed mothers sometimes insist on selecting their own partners. Women also influence the marriages of their daughters and granddaughters, especially when the selected husband dies before the bestowed child moves to his camp.

Among the Eskimo, representative of the rarest type of forager society, inequality between the sexes is matched by inequality in supplying the group with food. Inland Eskimo men hunt caribou throughout the year to provision the entire society, and maritime Eskimo men depend on whaling, fishing, and some hunting to feed their extended families. The women process the carcasses, cut and sew skins to make clothing, cook, and care for the young; but they collect no food of their own and depend on the men to supply all the raw materials for their work. Since men provide all the meat, they also control the trade in hides, whale oil, seal oil, and other items that move between the maritime and inland Eskimos.

Eskimo women are treated almost exclusively as objects to be used, abused, and traded by men. After puberty all Eskimo girls are fair game for any interested male. A man shows his intentions by grabbing the belt of a woman and if she protests, he cuts off her trousers and forces himself upon her. These encounters are considered unimportant by the rest of the group. Men offer their wives' sexual services to establish alliances with trading partners and members of hunting and whaling parties.

Despite the consistent pattern of some degree of male dominance among foragers, most of these societies are egalitarian compared with agricultural and industrial societies. No forager has any significant opportunity for political leadership. Foragers, as a rule, do not like to give or take orders, and assume leadership only with reluctance. Shamans (those who are thought to be possessed by spirits) may be either male or female. Public rituals conducted by women in order to celebrate the first menstruation of girls are common, and the symbolism in these rituals is similar to that in the ceremonies that follow a boy's first kill.

In any society, status goes to those who control the distribution of valued goods and services outside the family. Equality arises when both sexes work side by side in food production, as do the Washo, and the products are simply distributed among the workers. In such circumstances, no person or sex has greater access to valued items than do others. But when women make no contribution to the food supply, as in the case of the Eskimo, they are completely subordinate.

When we attempt to apply these generalizations to contemporary industrial society, we can predict that as long as women spend their discretionary income from jobs on domestic needs, they will gain little social recognition and power. To be an effective source of power, money must be exchanged in ways that require returns and create obligations. In other words, it must be invested.

Jobs that do not give women control over valued resources will do little to advance their general status. Only as managers, executives, and professionals are women in a position to trade goods and services, to do others favors, and therefore to obligate others to them. Only as controllers of valued resources can women achieve prestige, power, and equality.

Within the household, women who bring in income from jobs are able to function on a more nearly equal basis with their husbands. Women who contribute services to their husbands and children without pay, as do some middle-class Western housewives, are especially vulnerable to dominance. Like Eskimo women, as long as their services are limited to domestic distribution they have little power relative to their husbands and none with respect to the outside world.

As for the limits imposed on women by their procreative functions in hunter-gatherer societies, childbearing and child care are organized around work as much as work is organized around reproduction. Some foraging groups space their children three to four years apart and have an average of only four to six children, far fewer than many women in other cultures. Hunter-gatherers nurse their infants for extended periods, sometimes for as long as four years. This custom suppresses ovulation and limits the size of their families. Sometimes, although rarely, they practice infanticide. By limiting reproduction, a woman who is gathering food has only one child to carry.

Different societies can and do adjust the frequency of birth and the care of children to accommodate whatever productive activities women customarily engage in. In horticultural societies, where women work long hours in gardens that may be far from home, infants get food to supplement their mothers' milk, older children take care of younger children, and pregnancies are widely spaced. Throughout the world, if a society requires a woman's labor, it finds ways to care for her children.

In the United States, as in some other industrial societies, the accelerated entry of women with preschool children into the labor force has resulted in the development of a variety of child-care arrangements. Individual women have called on friends, relatives, and neighbors. Public and private child-care centers are growing. We should realize that the declining birth rate, the increasing acceptance of childless or single-child families, and a de-emphasis on motherhood are adaptations to a sexual division of labor reminiscent of the system of production found in hunter-gatherer societies.

In many countries where women no longer devote most of their productive years to childbearing, they are beginning to demand a change in the social relationship of the sexes. As women gain access to positions that control the exchange of resources, male dominance may become archaic, and industrial societies may one day become as egalitarian as the Washo.

DISCUSSION QUESTIONS

1. How does Professor Friedl explain the pervasive inequality between men and women found in the world today?
2. Which societies does Friedl cite as having relative gender equality and which societies does she cite as having high levels of inequality?
3. Based on her cross-cultural findings, what suggestions does Friedl make for Western women to acquire greater power and status?

RESOURCES ON THE INTERNET

InfoTrac College Edition

(http://infotrac.thomsonlearning.com/index.html)

You can find further relevant readings by searching *InfoTrac College Edition,* an online library with access to thousands of scholarly and popular periodicals. Below are suggested search terms for this article:

- gender inequality
- sex roles
- patriarchy

Anthropology Online: Wadsworth's Anthropology Resource Center

(http://anthropology.wadsworth.com)

The Wadsworth Anthropology Resource Center contains a wealth of information and useful tools for students including information on careers in anthropology.

9

Women and Men in !Kung Society

MARJORIE SHOSTAK

This selection on gender roles among the !Kung of Botswana is taken from Shostak's Nisa: The Life and Words of a !Kung Woman, *an interesting collaboration between ethnographer and informant. Each of the fifteen chapters in the book begins with an ethnographic description of a particular aspect of !Kung culture written by Shostak. The second part of each chapter is a monologue on the subject by Shostak's main informant, Nisa, in her own words. A particularly rich source of cultural information, Nisa was a gifted storyteller willing to describe her own life in great detail and on a variety of topics. She was first married at age twelve, was separated, divorced, remarried, widowed, and gave birth to four children. The result of this collaboration between ethnographer and informant is a vivid account of !Kung life told from a very personal perspective.*

Residing in the Kalahari Desert, Nisa belongs to one of the last hunting and gathering societies in the world, although within the last several decades many have taken to horticulture and the keeping of small herds of goats. Known for hundreds of years as the !Kung or the !Kung Bushmen, they are today referred to as Ju/'hoansi. As a people they have very distinguishable physical features, including light skin, high cheek bones, and an average height of approximately five feet.

After Besa and I had lived together for a long time, he went to visit some people in the East. While there, he found work with a Tswana cattle herder. When he came back, he told me to pack; he wanted me to go and live with him there. So we left and took the long trip to Old Debe's village, a Zhun/twa village near a Tswana and European settlement. We lived there together for a long time.[1]

While we were there, my father died. My older brother, my younger brother, and my mother were with him when he died, but I wasn't; I was living where Besa had taken me. Others carried the news to me. They said that Dau had tried to cure my father, laying on hands and working hard to make him better. But God refused and Dau wasn't able to see what was causing the illness so he could heal him. Dau said, "God is refusing to give up my father."

I heard and said, "Eh, then today I'm going to see where he died." Besa and I and my children, along with a few others, left to take the long journey west. We walked the first day and slept that night. The next morning we started out and slept again that night; we slept another night on the road, as well. As we walked, I cried and thought, "Why couldn't I have been with him when he died?" I cried as we walked, one day and the next and the next.

The sun was so hot, it was burning; it was killing us. One day we rested such a long time, I thought, "Is the sun going to stop me from seeing where my father died?" When it was cooler, we started walking again and slept on the road again that night.

We arrived at the village late in the afternoon. My younger brother, Kumsa, was the first to see us. When he saw me, he came and hugged me. We started to cry and cried together for a long time. Finally, our older brother stopped us, "That's enough for now. Your tears won't make our father alive again."

We stopped crying and we all sat down. My mother was also with us. Although my father never took her back again after the time she ran away with her lover, she returned and lived near him until he died. And even though she slept alone, she still loved him.

Later, my mother and I sat together and cried together.

We stayed there for a while, then Besa and I went back again to live in the East where he had been working for the Europeans. A very long time passed. Then, my brother sent word that my mother was dying. Once again we made the journey to my family and when we arrived I saw her: she was still alive.

We stayed there and lived there. One day, a group of people were going to the bush to live. I said, "Mother, come with us. I'll take care of you and can help me with my children." We traveled that day and slept that night; we traveled another day and slept another night. But the next night, the sickness that had been inside her grabbed her again and this time, held on. It was just as it had been with my father. The next day, she coughed up blood. I thought, "Oh, why is blood coming out like that? Is this what is going to kill her? Is this the way she's going to die? What is this sickness going to do? She's coughing blood . . . she's already dead!" Then I thought, "If only Dau were here, he would be able to cure her. He would trance for her every day." But he and my younger brother had stayed behind. Besa was with us, but he didn't have the power to cure people. There were others with us as well, but they didn't help.

We slept again that night. The next morning, the others left, as is our custom, and then it was only me, my children, my husband, and my mother; we were the only ones who remained. But her life was really over by then, even though she was still alive.

I went to get her some water and when I came back, she said, "Nisa . . . Nisa . . . I am an old person and today, my heart . . . today you and I will stay together for a while longer; we will continue to sit beside each other. But later, when the sun stands over there in the afternoon sky and when the new slim moon first strikes, I will leave you. We will separate then and I will go away."

I asked, "Mother, what are you saying?" She said, "Yes, that's what I'm saying. I am an old person. Don't deceive yourself; I am dying. When the sun moves to that spot in the sky, that will be our final separation. We will no longer be together after that. So, take good care of your children."

I said, "Why are you talking like this? If you die as you say, because that's what you're telling me, who are you going to leave in your place?" She said, "Yes, I am leaving you. Your husband will take care of you now. Besa will be with you and your children."

We remained together the rest of the day as the sun crawled slowly across the sky. When it reached the spot she had spoken of, she said—just like a person in good health—"Mm, now . . . be well, all of you," and then she died.

That night I slept alone and cried and cried and cried. None of my family was with me[2] and I just cried the entire night. When morning came, Besa dug a grave and buried her. I said, "Let's pull our things together and go back to the village. I want to tell Dau and Kumsa that our mother has died."

We walked that day and slept that night. We walked the next day and stopped again that night. The next morning, we met my brother Kumsa. Someone had told him that his mother was sick. When he heard, he took his bow and quiver and came looking for us. He left when the sun just rose and started walking toward us, even as we were walking toward him. We met when the sun was overhead. He stood and looked at me. Then he said, "Here you are, Nisa, with your son and your daughter and your husband. But Mother isn't with you. . . ."

I sat down and started to cry. He said. "Mother must have died because you're crying like this," and he started to cry, too. Besa said, "Yes, your sister left your mother behind. Two days ago was when your mother and sister separated. That is where we are coming from now. Your sister is here and will tell you about it. You will be together to share your mourning for your mother. That will be good."

We stayed there and cried and cried. Later, Kumsa took my little son and carried him on his shoulders. I carried my daughter and we walked until we arrived back at the village. My older brother came with his wife, and when he saw us he, too, started to cry.

After that, we lived together for a while. I lived and cried, lived and cried. My mother had been so beautiful . . . her face, so lovely. When she died, she caused me great pain. Only after a long time was I quiet again.

Before we returned to the East, I went with Besa to visit his family. While I was there, I became very sick. It came from having carried my mother. Because when she was sick, I carried her around on my back. After she died, my back started to hurt in the very place I had carried her. One of God's spiritual arrows must have struck me there and found its way into my chest.

I was sick for a long time and then blood started to come out of my mouth. My younger brother (he really loves me!) was visiting me at the time. When he saw how I was, he left to tell his older brother, "Nisa's dying the same way our mother died. I've come to tell you to come back with me and heal her." My older brother listened and the two of them traveled to where I was. They came when the sun was high in the afternoon sky. Dau started to trance for me. He laid on hands, healing me with his touch. He worked on me for a long time. Soon, I was able to sleep; then, the blood stopped coming from my chest and later, even if I coughed, there wasn't any more blood.

We stayed there for a few more days. Then, Dau said, "Now I'm going to take Nisa with me to my village." Besa agreed and we all left together. We stayed at my brother's village until I was completely better.

Besa and I eventually moved back East again. But after we had lived together for a long time, we no longer were getting along. One day I asked, "Besa, won't you take me back to my family's village so I can live there?" He said, "I'm no longer interested in you." I said, "What's wrong? Why do you feel that way?" But then I said, "Eh, if that's how it is, it doesn't matter."

I was working for a European woman at the time, and when I told her what Besa was saying to me, she told him, "Listen to me. You're going to chase your wife away. If you continue to speak to her like this, she'll be gone. Today, I'm pregnant. Why don't you just let her be and have her sit beside you. When I give birth, she will work for me and help me with the baby."

That's what we did. We continued to live together until she gave birth. After, I helped wash the baby's clothes and helped with other chores. I worked for her for a long time.

One day, Besa broke into a little box I had and stole the money she had paid me with. He took it and went to drink beer. I went to the European woman and told her Besa had taken five Rand[3] from me and had left with it. I asked her to help me get it back. We went to the Tswana but where everyone was drinking and went to the door. The European woman walked in, kicked over a bucket and the beer spilled out. She kicked over another and another and the beer was spilling everywhere. The Tswanas left. She turned to Besa and said, "Why are you treating this young Zhun/twa woman like this? Stop treating her this way." She told him to give her the money and when he gave it to her, she gave it to me. I went and put the money in the box, then took it and left it in her kitchen where it stayed.

Later Besa said, "Why did you tell on me? I'm going to beat you." I said, "Go ahead. Hit me. I don't care. I won't stop you."

Soon after that, I became pregnant with Besa's child. But when it was still very tiny, when

I was still carrying it way inside, he left me. I don't know what it was that made him want to leave. Did he have a lover? I don't know. He said he was afraid of a sore I had on my face where a bug had bitten me. It had become swollen, and eventually the Europeans helped to heal it. Whatever it was, his heart had changed toward me and although my heart still liked him, he only liked me a very little then. That's why he left.

It happened the day he finished working for the Europeans. He came back when the sun was low in the sky and said, "Tomorrow, I'm going to visit my younger brother. I have finished my work and have been paid. I'm going, but you'll stay here. Later, Old Debe and his wife can take you back to your brothers' village." I said, "If you are leaving, won't I go with you?" He said, "No, you won't go with me." I said, "Why are you saying you'll go without me? If I go with you and give birth there, it will be good. Don't leave me here. Let me go with you and give birth in your brother's village." But he said, "No, Old Debe will bring you back to your family."

When I saw Old Debe, he asked me what was wrong. I said, "What is Besa doing to me? If he doesn't want me, why doesn't he just end it completely? I've seen for a long time that he doesn't want me." I thought, "Besa . . . he took me to this faraway village, got me pregnant, and now, is he just going to drop me in this foreign place where none of my people live?"

Later, I said to Besa, "Why did you take me from my people? My brothers are still alive, yet you won't take me to them. You say someone else will. But, why should someone else, a near stranger, take me to my family after you've given me this stomach. I say you should take me to them, take me there and say, 'Here is your sister. Today I am separating from her.' Instead, you're saying you'll just leave me here, with these strangers? I followed you here, to where you were working, because you wanted me to. Now you're just going to leave me? Why are you doing this? Can there be any good in it?"

I continued, "You're the one who came here to work. Yet, you have no money and have no blankets. But when you had no more work and no more money, I worked. I alone, a woman. I entered the work of the European and I alone bought us blankets and a trunk. I alone bought all those things and you covered yourself with my blankets. When you weren't working, you asked people to give you things. How can you leave me here in this foreign place after all that?" He answered, "What work could I have done when there wasn't any to be had?"

I said, "It doesn't matter, because I can see that you will only be here for a few more nights, then you will go. I know that now. But, if you leave me like this today, then tomorrow, after you have gone and have lived with your brother, if you ever decide to come to where I am living, I will refuse you and will no longer be your wife. Because you are leaving me when I am pregnant."

The next morning, early, he tied up his things and left. He packed everything from inside the hut, including all our blankets, and went to his brother's village to live. I thought, "Eh, it doesn't matter, after all. I'll just sit here and let him go." He left me with nothing; the people in the village had to give me blankets to sleep with.

Besa, that man is very bad. He left me hanging like that.

Once he left, I saw that I would be staying there for a while. I thought, "Today I'm no longer going to refuse other men, but will just be with them. Then, maybe I will miscarry. Because this is Besa's child and didn't he leave it and go? I won't refuse other men and will just have them. I will drop this pregnancy; then I will go home."

That's when Numshe entered the hut with me. He spoke to me and I agreed. People said, "Yes, she will enter the hut with him. But when he tastes her,[4] the pregnancy will be ruined." Old Debe's wife said, "That won't be so bad. If her pregnancy is ruined, it won't be a bad thing. Because Besa dropped her. Therefore, I will sit here and take care of her. Later, I will bring her to her family."

I lived there for a long time. I lived alone and worked for the Europeans. Then one day, just as my heart had said, my body felt like fire and my stomach was in great pain. I told Old Debe's wife, "Eh-hey, today I'm sick." She asked, "Where does it hurt? Do you want some water? Where is the sickness hurting you." I said, "My whole body hurts, it isn't just my stomach." I lay there and felt the pains, rising again and again and again. I thought, "That man certainly has made me feel bad; even today, I'm lying here in great pain."

She looked at my stomach and saw how it was standing out. She said, "Oh, my child. Are you going to drop your pregnancy? What is going to happen? Will you be able to give birth to this child or will it be a miscarriage? Here, there are just the two of us; I don't see anyone who will bring more help to you. If you miscarry, it will be only us two." I said, "Yes, that's fine. If I drop this pregnancy, it will be good. I want to drop it, then I can leave. Because my husband certainly doesn't want it."

We stayed together all day. When the sun was late in the sky, I told her it was time and we went together to the bush. I sat down and soon the baby was born. It was already big, with a head and arms and a little penis; but it was born dead. Perhaps my heart had ruined my pregnancy. I cried, "This man almost ruined me, did he not?" Debe's wife said, "Yes, he destroyed this baby, this baby which came from God. But if God hadn't been here helping you, you also would have died. Because when a child dies in a woman's stomach, it can kill the woman. But God . . . God gave you something beautiful in giving you this baby and although it had death in it, you yourself are alive." We left and walked back to the village. Then I lay down.

After that, I just continued to live there. One day I saw people visiting from Besa's village. I told them to tell him that our marriage had ended. I said, "Tell him that he shouldn't think, even with a part of his heart, that he still has a wife here or that when we meet another time in my village that he might still want me." That's what I said and that's what I thought.

Because he left me there to die.

Soon after, a man named Twi saw me and said, "Did your husband leave you?" I said, "Yes, he left me long ago." He asked, "Then won't you stay with me?" I refused the first time he asked as well as the second and the third. But when he asked the next time, I agreed and we started to live together. I continued to work for the European woman until my work was finished and she told me I could go home. She gave us food for our trip and then all of us—Old Debe, his wife; Twi, and me—traveled the long distance back to where my family was living.

Twi and I lived together in my brothers' village for a long time. Then, one day, Besa came from wherever he had been and said, "Nisa, I've come to take you back with me." I said, "What? What am I like today? Did I suddenly become beautiful? The way I used to be is the way I am now; the way I used to be is what you left behind when you dropped me. So what are you saying? First you drop me in the heart of where the white people live, then you come back and say I should once again be with you?" He said, "Yes, we will pick up our marriage again."

I was stunned! I said, "What are you talking about? This man, Twi, helped bring me back. He's the man who will marry me. You're the one who left me." We talked until he could say nothing more; he was humbled. Finally he said, "You're shit! That's what you are." I said, "I'm shit you say? That's what you thought about me long ago, and I knew it. That's why I told you while we were still living in the Fast that I wanted you to take me back to my family so we could end our marriage here. But today, I came here myself and you only came afterward. Now I refuse to have anything more to do with you."

That's when Besa brought us to the Tswana headman to ask for a tribal hearing. Once it started, the headman looked at everything. He asked me, "Among all the women who live here, among all those you see sitting around, do you see one who lives with two men?" I said, "No, the women who sit here . . . not one lives with two men; not one among them would I be able to find. I, alone, have two. But it was because this man, Besa, mistreated and hurt me. That's why I took this other man, Twi, who treats me well, who does things for me and gives me things to eat." Then I said, "He is also the man I want to marry; I want to drop the other one. Because Besa has no sense. He left me while I was pregnant and the pregnancy almost killed me. This other one is the one I want to marry."

We talked a long time. Finally, the headman told Besa, "I have questioned Nisa about what happened and she has tied you up with her talk; her talk has defeated you, without doubt. Because what she has said about her pregnancy is serious. Therefore, today she and Twi will continue to stay together. After more time passes, I will ask all of you to come back again." Later, Twi and I left and went back to my brothers' village to sleep.

The next day, my older brother saw a honey cache while walking in the bush. He came to tell us and take us back there with him; we planned to stay the night in the bush. We arrived and spent the rest of the day collecting honey. When we finished, we walked toward where we were planning to camp. That's when I saw Besa's tracks in the sand. I said, "Everyone! Come here! Besa's tracks are here! Has anyone seen them elsewhere?" One of the men said, "Nonsense! Would you know his tracks . . . ." I interrupted, "My husband . . . the man who married me. . . . I *know* his tracks." The man's wife came to look, "Yes, those are Besa's tracks; his wife really did see them.

The next morning, Besa walked into the camp. Besa and Twi started to fight. My older brother yelled, "Do you two want to kill Nisa? Today she is not taking another husband. Today she's just going to lie by herself." I agreed, "Eh, I don't want to marry again now."

Twi and I continued to live together after that. But later we separated. My older brother caused it, because he wanted Besa to be with me again. He liked him and didn't like Twi. That's why he forced Twi to leave. When Twi saw how much anger both Dau and Besa felt toward him, he became afraid, and finally he left.

I saw what my brother had done and was miserable; I had really liked Twi. I said, "So, this is what you wanted? Fine, but now that you have chased Twi away, I'll have nothing at all to do with Besa." That's when I began to refuse Besa completely. Besa went to the headman and said, "Nisa refuses to be with me." The headman said, "Nisa's been refusing you for a long time. What legal grounds could I possibly find for you now?"

After more time passed, a man who had been my lover years before, started with me again. Soon we were very much in love. He was so handsome! His nose . . . his eyes . . . everything was so beautiful! His skin was light and his nose was lovely. I really loved that man, even when I first saw him.

We lived together for a while, but then he died. I was miserable, "My lover has died. Where am I going to find another like him—another as beautiful, another as good, another with a European nose and with such lovely light skin? Now he's dead. Where will I ever find another like him?"

My heart was miserable and I mourned for him. I exhausted myself with mourning and only when it was finished did I feel better again.

After years of living and having everything that happened to me happen, that's when I started with Bo, the next important man in my life and the one I am married to today.

Besa and I lived separately, but he still wanted me and stayed near me. That man, he didn't hear; he didn't understand. He was without ears, because he still said, "This woman here, Nisa, I won't be finished with her."

People told Bo, "You're going to die. This man, Besa, he's going to kill you. Now, leave Nisa." But Bo refused, "Me . . . I won't go to another hut. I'll just stay with Nisa and even if Besa tries to kill me, I'll still be here and won't leave."

At first, Bo and I sneaked off together, but Besa suspected us; he was very jealous. He accused me all the time. Even when I just went to urinate, he'd say that I had been with Bo. Or when I went for water, he'd say, "Did you just meet your lover?" But I'd say, "What makes you think you can talk to me like that?" He'd say, "Nisa are you not still my wife? Why aren't we living together? What are you doing?" I'd say,

"Don't you have other women or are they refusing you, too? You have others so why are you asking me about what I'm doing?"

One night, Bo and I were lying down inside my hut and as I looked out through the latched-branch door, I saw someone moving about. It was Besa; I was able to see his face. He wanted to catch us, hoping I would feel some remorse and perhaps return to him.

I said, "What? Besa's here! Bo . . . Bo . . . Besa's standing out there." Bo got up; Besa came and stood by the door. I got up and that's when Besa came in and grabbed me. He held onto me and threatened to throw me into the fire. I cursed him as he held me, "Besa-Big-Testicles! Long-Penis! First you left me and drank of women's genitals elsewhere. Now you come back, see me, and say I am your wife?" He pushed me toward the fire, but I twisted my body so I didn't land in it. Then he went after Bo. Bo is weaker and older than Besa, so Besa was able to grab him, pull him outside the hut, and throw him down. He bit him on the shoulder. Bo yelled out in pain.

My younger brother woke and ran to us, yelling, "Curses to your genitals!" He grabbed them and separated them. Bo cursed Besa. Besa cursed Bo, "Curses on your penis!" He yelled, "I'm going to kill you Bo, then Nisa will suffer! If I don't kill you, then maybe I'll kill her so that you will feel pain! Because what you have that is so full of pleasure, I also have. So why does her heart want you and refuse me?"

I yelled at him, "That's not it! It's you! It's who you are and the way you think! This one, Bo, his ways are good and his thoughts are good. But you, your ways are foul. Look, you just bit Bo; that, too, is part of your ways. You also left me to die. And death, that's something I'm afraid of. That's why you no longer have a hold over me. Today I have another who will take care of me well. I'm no longer married to you, Besa. I want my husband to be Bo."

Besa kept bothering me and hanging around me. He'd ask, "Why won't you come to me? Come to me, I'm a man. Why are you afraid of me?" I wouldn't answer. Once Bo answered. "I don't understand why, if you *are* a man, you keep pestering this woman? Is what you're doing going to do any good? Because I won't leave her. And even though you bit me and your marks are on me, you're the one who is going to move out of the way, not me. I intend to marry her."

Another time I told Bo, "Don't be afraid of Besa. You and I will marry; I'm not going to stay married to him. Don't let him frighten you. Because even if he comes here with arrows, he won't do anything with them." Bo said, "Even if he did, what good would that do? I am also a man and am a master of arrows. The two of us would just strike each other. That's why I keep telling him to let you go; I am the man you are with now."

The next time, Besa came with his quiver full of arrows, saying, "I'm going to get Nisa and bring her back with me." He left with another man and came to me at my village. When he arrived, the sun was high in the sky. I was resting. He said, "Nisa, come, let's go." I said, "What? Is your penis not well? Is it horny?"

People heard us fighting and soon everyone was there, my younger and older brothers as well. Besa and I kept arguing and fighting until, in a rage, I screamed, "All right! Today I'm no longer afraid!" and I pulled off all the skins that were covering me—first one, then another, and finally the leather apron that covered my genitals. I pulled them all off and laid them down on the ground. I cried, "There! There's my vagina! Look, Besa, look at me! This is what you want!"

The man he had come with said, "This woman, her heart is truly far from you. Besa, look. Nisa refuses you totally, with all her heart. She refuses to have sex with you. Your relationship with her is finished. See. She took off her clothes, put them down, and with her genitals is showing everyone how she feels about you. She doesn't want you, Besa. If I were you, I'd finish with her today." Besa finally said, "Eh, you're right. Now I am finished with her."

The two of them left. I took my leather apron, put it on, took the rest of my things and put them on.

Mother! That was just what I did.

Besa tried one last time. He went to the headman again, and when he came back he told me, "The headman wants to see you." I thought, "If he wants to see me, I won't refuse."

When I arrived, the headman said, "Besa says he still wants to continue your marriage." I said, "Continue our marriage? Why? Am I so stupid that I don't know my name? Would I stay in a marriage with a man who left me hanging in a foreign place? If Old Debe and his wife hadn't been there, I would have truly lost my way. Me, stay married to Besa? I can't make myself think of it."

I turned to Besa, "Isn't that what I told you when we were still in the East?" Besa said, "Mm, that's what you said." I said, "And, when you left, didn't I tell you that you were leaving me pregnant with your baby. Didn't I also tell you that?" He said, "Yes, that's what you said." I said, "And didn't I say that I wanted to go with you, that I wanted you to help make our pregnancy grow strong? Didn't I say that and didn't you refuse?" He said, "Yes, you said that." Then I said, "Mm. Therefore, that marriage you say today, in the lap of the headman, should be continued, that marriage no longer exists. Because I am Nisa and today, when I look at you, all I want to do is to throw up. Vomit is the only thing left in my heart for you now. As we sit together here and I see your face, that is all that rises within and grabs me."

The headman laughed, shook his head and said, "Nisa is impossible!" Then he said, "Besa, you had better listen to her. Do you hear what she is saying? She says that you left her while she was pregnant, that she miscarried and was miserable. Today she will no longer take you for her husband." Besa said, "That's because she's with Bo now and doesn't want to leave him. But I still want her and want to continue our marriage."

I said, "What? Besa, can't you see me? Can't you see that I have really found another man? Did you think, perhaps, that I was too old and wouldn't find someone else?" The headman laughed again. "Yes, I am a woman. And that which you have, a penis, I also have something of equal worth. Like the penis of a chief . . . yes, something of a chief is what I have. And its worth is like money. Therefore, the person who drinks from it . . . it's like he's getting money from me. But not you, because when you had it, you just left it to ruin."

The headman said, "Nisa is crazy; her talk is truly crazy now." Then he said, "The two of you sleep tonight and give your thoughts over to this. Nisa, think about all of it again. Tomorrow, I want both of you to come back."

Besa went and lay down. I went and lay down and thought about everything. In the morning, I went to the headman. I felt ashamed by my talk of the night before. I sat there quietly. The headman said, "Nisa, Besa says you should stay married to him." I answered, "Why should he stay married to me when yesterday I held his baby in my stomach and he dropped me. Even God doesn't want me to marry a man who leaves me, a man who takes my blankets when I have small children beside me, a man who forces other people to give me blankets to cover my children with. Tell him to find another woman to marry."

The headman turned to Besa, "Nisa has explained herself. There's nothing more I can see to say. Even you, you can hear that she has defeated you. So, leave Nisa and as I am headman, today your marriage to her is ended. She can now marry Bo."[5]

Besa went to the headman one more time. When he tried to discuss it again, saying, "Please, help me. Give Nisa back to me," the headman said, "Haven't you already talked to me about this? You talked and talked, and the words entered my ears. Are you saying that I have not already decided on this? That I am not an important person? That I am a worthless thing that you do not have to listen to? There is no reason to give Nisa back to you."

I was so thankful when I heard his words. My heart filled with happiness.

Bo and I married soon after that.[6] We lived together, sat together, and did things together. Our hearts loved each other very much and our marriage was very very strong.

Besa also married again not long after—this time to a woman much younger than me. One day he came to me and said, "Look how wrong you were to have refused me! Perhaps you thought you were the only woman. But you, Nisa, today you are old and you yourself can see that I have married a young woman, one who is beautiful!"

I said, "Good! I told you that if we separated, you'd find a young woman to marry and to sleep with. That is fine with me because there is nothing I want from you. But you know, of course, that just like me, another day she too will be old."

We lived on, but not long after, Besa came back. He said that his young wife was troubled and that he wanted me again. I refused and even told Bo about it. Bo asked me why I refused. I said, "Because I don't want him." But what he says about his wife is true. She has a terrible sickness, a type of madness. God gave it to her. She was such a beautiful woman, too. But no longer. I wonder why such a young woman has to have something like that. . . .

Even today, whenever Besa sees me, he argues with me and says he still wants me. I say, "Look, we've separated. Now leave me alone." I even sometimes refuse him food. Bo tells me I shouldn't refuse, but I'm afraid he will bother me more if I give anything to him. Because his heart still cries for me.

Sometimes I do give him things to eat and he also gives things to me. Once I saw him in my village. He came over to me and said, "Nisa, give me some water to drink." I washed out a cup and poured him some water. He drank it and said, "Now, give me some tobacco." I took out some tobacco and gave it to him. Then he said, "Nisa, you really are adult; you know how to work. Today, I am married to a woman but my heart doesn't agree to her much. But you . . . you are one who makes me feel pain. Because you left me and married another man. I also married, but have made myself weary by having married something bad. You, you have hands that work and do things. With you, I could eat: You would get water for me to wash with. Today, I'm really in pain."

I said, "Why are you thinking about our dead marriage? Of course, we were married once, but we have gone our different ways. Now, I no longer want you. After all that happened when you took me East—living there, working there, my father dying, my mother dying, and all the misery you caused me—you say we should live together once again?"

He said that I wasn't telling it as it happened.

One day, he told me he wanted to take me from Bo. I said, "What? Tell me, Besa, what has been talking to you that you are saying this again?" He said, "All right, then have me as your lover. Won't you help my heart out?" I said, "Aren't there many men who could be my lover? Why should I agree to you?" He said, "Look here, Nisa . . . I'm a person who helped bring up your children, the children you and your husband gave birth to. You became pregnant again with my child and that was good. You held it inside you and lived with it until God came and killed it. That's why your heart is talking this way and refusing me."

I told him he was wrong. But he was right, too. Because, after Besa, I never had any more children. He took that away from me. With Tashay, I had children, but Besa, he ruined me. Even the one time I did conceive, I miscarried. That's because of what he did to me; that's what everyone says.

NOTES

1. This chapter covers about five years, beginning when Nisa was in her early thirties (c. the mid 1950s).
2. In fact, her husband and children were with her.

3. The Rand is a South African currency that was then legal tender in Bechuanaland (pre-independence Botswana). It was worth between $1.20 and $1.50. Five Rand was a very large sum of money to the !Kung at that time—perhaps as much as two months wages at a typical menial task.
4. Tastes her: A euphemism for sexual intercourse.
5. The procedure for divorce in traditional !Kung culture would have been less complicated and would have proceeded more quickly.
6. Nisa and Bo married around 1957, when Nisa was about thirty-six years old.

DISCUSSION QUESTION

1. Based on this account, would you say that women are an exploited, low-status segment of !Kung society?

RESOURCES ON THE INTERNET

InfoTrac College Edition

(http://infotrac.thomsonlearning.com/index.html)

You can find further relevant readings by searching *InfoTrac College Edition,* an online library with access to thousands of scholarly and popular periodicals. Below are suggested search terms for this article:

- life story
- remarriage

Anthropology Online: Wadsworth's Anthropology Resource Center

(http://anthropology.wadsworth.com)

The Wadsworth Anthropology Resource Center contains a wealth of information and useful tools for students including information on careers in anthropology.

10

The Kpelle Moot

JAMES L. GIBBS, JR.

A cultural universal found in all societies of the world is the notion of social control. More specifically, no society can function for very long without some well-understood mechanisms for settling disputes. Some societies rely on formal mechanisms (such as courts of law), while others rely on more informal mechanisms, many of which have different purposes, procedures, and functionaries.

In this selection, anthropologist James Gibbs describes how informal, ad hoc mechanisms of conflict resolution (called "moots") operate among the Kpelle of Liberia. Found in many other areas of Africa as well, these moots are local phenomena in which kinsmen, neighbors, and friends come together to try to settle disputes and normalize relationships between the disputants. While moots coexist along with a more formal court system administered by political chiefs, there are some significant differences between the two types of adjudicating structures. Chiefly courts have as their major objective the administration of justice, whereby guilt is determined and an appropriate penalty is levied. Moots, on the other hand, are not primarily interested in making certain that the penalty fits the crime. Instead, moots are aimed at resolving disagreements, extracting apologies, imposing token penalties, normalizing good relationships between the disputants, and reintegrating them back into the community. Moots are particularly effective mechanisms for resolving local conflicts between people who are part of the same small-scale community. Thus, whereas the traditional courts tend to be more coercive and punitive, the Kpelle moots are more conciliatory and therapeutic in nature.

Africa as a major culture area has been characterized by many writers as being marked by a high development of law and legal procedures.[1] In the past few years research on African law has produced a series of highly competent monographs such as those on law among the Tiv, the Barotse, and the Nuer.[2] These and related shorter studies have focused primarily on formal processes for the settlement of disputes, such as those which take place in a courtroom, or those which are, in some other way, set apart from simpler measures of social control. However,

From "The Kpelle Moot" by James L. Gibbs, Jr. in *Africa* 33(1), January 1963. Reprinted by permission from the author.

many African societies have informal, quasi-legal, dispute-settlement procedures, supplemental to formal ones, which have not been as well studied, or—in most cases—adequately analysed.

In this paper I present a description and analysis of one such institution for the informal settlement of disputes, as it is found among the Kpelle of Liberia; it is the moot, the *bɛrɛi mu meni saa* or "house palaver." Hearings in the Kpelle moot contrast with those in a court in that they differ in tone and effectiveness. The genius of the moot lies in the fact that it is based on a covert application of the principles of psychoanalytic theory which underlie psychotherapy.

The Kpelle are a Mande-speaking, patrilineal group of some 175,000 rice cultivators who live in Central Liberia and the adjoining regions of Guinea. This paper is based on data gathered in a field study which I carried out in 1957 and 1958 among the Liberian Kpelle of Panta Chiefdom in north-east Central Province.

Strong corporate patrilineages are absent among the Kpelle. The most important kinship group is the virilocal polygynous family which sometimes becomes an extended family, almost always of the patrilineal variety. Several of these families form the core of a residential group, known as a village quarter, more technically, a clan-barrio.[3] This is headed by a quarter elder who is related to most of the household heads by real or putative patrilineal ties.

Kpelle political organization is centralized although there is no single king or paramount chief, but a series of chiefs of the same level of authority, each of whom is superordinate over district chiefs and town chiefs. Some political functions are also vested in the tribal fraternity, the Poro, which still functions vigorously. The form of political organization found in the area can thus best be termed the polycephalous associational state.

The structure of the Kpelle court system parallels that of the political organization. In Liberia the highest court of a tribal authority and the highest tribal court chartered by the Government is that of a paramount chief. A district chief's court is also an official court. Disputes may be settled in these official courts or in unofficial courts, such as those of town chiefs or quarter elders. In addition to this, grievances are settled informally in moots, and sometimes by associational groupings such as church councils or cooperative work groups.

In my field research I studied both the formal and informal methods of dispute settlement. The method used was to collect case material in as complete a form as possible. Accordingly, immediately after a hearing, my interpreter and I would prepare verbatim transcripts of each case that we heard. These transcripts were supplemented with accounts—obtained from respondents—of past cases or cases which I did not hear litigated. Transcripts from each type of hearing were analysed phrase by phrase in terms of a frame of reference derived from jurisprudence and ethno-law. The results of the analysis indicate two things: first, that courtroom hearings and moots are quite different in their procedures and tone, and secondly, why they show this contrast.

Kpelle courtroom hearings are basically coercive and arbitrary in tone. In another paper[4] I have shown that this is partly the result of the intrusion of the authoritarian values of the Poro into the courtroom. As a result, the court is limited in the manner in which it can handle some types of disputes. The court is particularly effective in settling cases such as assault, possession of illegal charms, or theft where the litigants are not linked in a relationship which must continue after the trial. However, most of the cases brought before a Kpelle court are cases involving disputed rights over women, including matrimonial matters which are usually cast in the form of suits for divorce. The court is particularly inept at settling these numerous matrimonial disputes because its harsh tone tends to drive spouses farther apart rather than to reconcile them. The moot, in contrast, is more effective in handling such cases. The following analysis indicates the reasons for this.[5]

The Kpelle *bɛrɛi mu meni saa,* or "house palaver," is an informal airing of a dispute which takes place before an assembled group which includes kinsmen of the litigants and neighbors from the quarter where the case is being heard. It is a completely *ad hoc* group, varying greatly in composition from case to case. The matter to be settled is usually a domestic problem: alleged mistreatment or neglect by a spouse, an attempt to collect money paid to a kinsman for a job which was not completed, or a quarrel among brothers over the inheritance of their father's wives.

In the procedural description which follows I shall use illustrative data from the Case of the Ousted Wife:

> Wama Nya, the complainant, had one wife, Yua. His older brother died and he inherited the widow, Yokpo, who moved into his house. The two women were classificatory sisters. After Yokpo moved in, there was strife in the household. The husband accused her of staying out late at night, of harvesting rice without his knowledge, and of denying him food. He also accused Yokpo of having lovers and admitted having had a physical struggle with her, after which he took a basin of water and "washed his hands of her."
>
> Yokpo countered by denying the allegations about having lovers, saying that she was accused falsely, although she had in the past confessed the name of one lover. She further complained that Wama Nya had assaulted her and, in the act, had committed the indignity of removing her headtie, and had expelled her from the house after the ritual handwashing. Finally, she alleged that she had been thus cast out of the house at the instigation of the other wife who, she asserted, had great influence over their husband.
>
> Kɔlɔ Waa, the Town Chief and quarter elder, and the brother of Yokpo, was the mediator of the moot, which decided that the husband was mainly at fault, although Yua and Yokpo's children were also in the wrong. Those at fault had to apologize to Yokpo and bring gifts of apology as well as local rum[6] for the disputants and participants in the moot.

The moot is most often held on a Sunday—a day of rest for Christians and non-Christians alike—at the home of the complainant, the person who calls the moot. The mediator will have been selected by the complainant. He is a kinsman who also holds an office such as town chief or quarter elder, and therefore has some skill in dispute settlement. It is said that he is chosen to preside by virtue of his kin tie, rather than because of his office.

The proceedings begin with the pronouncing of blessings by one of the oldest men of the group. In the Case of the Ousted Wife, Gbenai Zua, the elder who pronounced the blessings, took a rice-stirrer in his hand and, striding back and forth, said:

> This man has called us to fix the matter between him and his wife. May ɑ*ala* (the supreme, creator deity) change his heart and let his household be in good condition. May ɑ*ala* bless the family and make them fruitful. May He bless them so they can have food this year. May He bless the children and the rest of the family so they may always be healthy. May He bless them to have good luck. When Wama Nya takes a gun and goes in the bush, may he kill big animals. May ɑ*ala* bless us to enjoy the meat. May He bless us to enjoy life and always have luck. May ɑ*ala* bless all those who come to discuss this matter.

The man who pronounces the blessings always carries a stick or a whisk *(kpung)* which he waves for effect as he paces up and down chanting his injunctions. Participation of spectators is demanded, for the blessings are chanted by the elder (*kpung namu* or "*kpung* owner") as a series of imperatives, some of which he repeats. Each phrase is responded to by the spectators who answer in unison with a formal response, either *e ka ti* (so be it), or a low, drawn-out *eeee.* The *kpung namu* delivers his blessings faster and faster, building up a rhythmic interaction pattern with the other participants The effect is to unite those attending in common action before the hearing begins. The blessing focuses attention on the concern with maintaining harmony and the well-being of the group as a whole.

Everyone attending the moot wears their next-to-best clothes or, if it is not Sunday, every-day clothes. Elders, litigants, and spectators sit in mixed fashion, pressed closely upon each other, often overflowing onto a veranda. This is in contrast to the vertical spatial separation between litigants and adjudicators in the courtroom. The mediator, even though he is a chief, does not wear his robes. He and the oldest men will be given chairs as they would on any other occasion.

The complainant speaks first and may be interrupted by the mediator or anyone else present. After he has been thoroughly quizzed, the accused will answer and will also be questioned by those present. The two parties will question each other directly and question others in the room also. Both the testimony and the questioning are lively and uninhibited. Where there are witnesses to some of the actions described by the parties, they may also speak and be questioned. Although the proceedings are spirited, they remain orderly. The mediator may fine anyone who speaks out of turn by requiring them to bring some rum for the group to drink.

The mediator and others present will point out the various faults committed by both the parties. After everyone has been heard, the mediator expresses the consensus of the group. For example, in the Case of the Ousted Wife, he said to Yua: "The words you used towards your sister were not good, so come and beg her pardon."

The person held to be mainly at fault will then formally apologize to the other person. This apology takes the form of the giving of token gifts to the wronged person by the guilty party. These may be an item of clothing, a few coins, clean hulled rice, or a combination of all three. It is also customary for the winning party in accepting the gifts of apology to give, in return, a smaller token such as a twenty-five cent piece[7] to show his "white heart" or good will. The losing party is also lightly "fined"; he must present rum or beer to the mediator and the others who heard the case. This is consumed by all in attendance. The old man then pronounces blessings again and offers thanks for the restoration of harmony within the group, and asks that all continue to act with good grace and unity.

An initial analysis of the procedural steps of the moot isolates the descriptive attributes of the moot and shows that they contrast with those of the courtroom hearing. While the airing of grievances is incomplete in courtroom hearings, it is more complete in the moot. This fuller airing of the issues results, in many marital cases, in a more harmonious solution. Several specific features of the house palaver facilitate this wider airing of grievances. First, the hearing takes place soon after a breach has occurred, before the grievances have hardened. There is no delay until the complainant has time to go to the paramount chief's or district chief's headquarters to institute suit. Secondly, the hearing takes place in the familiar surroundings of a home. The robes, writs, messengers, and other symbols of power which subtly intimidate and inhibit the parties in the courtroom, by reminding them of the physical force which underlies the procedures, are absent. Thirdly, in the courtroom the conduct of the hearing is firmly in the hands of the judge but in the moot the investigatory initiative rests much more with the parties themselves. Jurisprudence suggests that, in such a case, more of the grievances lodged between the parties are likely to be aired and adjusted. Finally, the range of relevance applied to matters which are brought out is extremely broad. Hardly anything mentioned is held to be irrelevant. This too leads to a more thorough ventilation of the issues.

There is a second surface difference between court and moot. In a courtroom hearing, the solution is, by and large, one which is imposed by the adjudicator. In the moot the solution is more consensual. It is, therefore, more likely to be accepted by both parties and hence more durable. Several features of the moot contribute to the consensual solution: first, there is no unilateral ascription of blame, but an attribution of fault to both parties. Secondly, the mediator, unlike the chief in the courtroom, is not backed by political authority and the physical force which underlies it. He cannot jail parties, nor can he levy a heavy fine. Thirdly, the sanctions which are imposed are not so burdensome as to cause hardship to the losing party or to give him or her grounds for a new grudge against the other party. The gifts for the winning party and the potables for the spectators are not as expensive as the fines and the court costs in a paramount chief's court. Lastly, the ritualized apology of the moot symbolizes very concretely the consensual nature of the solution.[8] The public offering and acceptance of the tokens of apology indicate that each party has no further grievances and that the settlement is satisfactory and mutually acceptable. The parties and spectators drink together to symbolize the restarted solidarity of the group and the rehabilitation of the offending party.

This type of analysis describes the courtroom hearing and the moot, using a frame of reference derived from jurisprudence and ethno-law which is explicitly comparative and evaluative. Only by using this type of comparative approach can the researcher select features of the hearings which are not only unique to each of them, but theoretically significant in that their contribution to the social-control functions of the proceedings can be hypothesized. At the same time, it enables the researcher to pin-point in procedures the cause for what he feels intuitively: that the two hearings contrast in tone, even though they are similar in some ways.

However, one can approach the transcripts of the trouble cases with a second analytical framework and emerge with a deeper understanding of the implications of the contrasting descriptive attributes of the court and the house palaver. Remember that the coercive tone of the courtroom hearing limits the court's effectiveness in dealing with matrimonial disputes, especially in effecting reconciliations. The moot, on the other hand, is particularly effective in bringing about reconciliations between spouses. This is because the moot is not only conciliatory, but *therapeutic.* Moot procedures are therapeutic in that, like psychotherapy, they re-educate the parties through a type of social learning brought about in a specially structured interpersonal setting.

Talcott Parsons[9] has written that therapy involves four elements: support, permissiveness, denial of reciprocity, and manipulation of rewards. Writers such as Frank,[10] Klapman,[11] and Opler[12] have pointed out that the same elements characterize not only individual psychotherapy, but group psychotherapy as well. All four elements are writ large in the Kpelle moot.

The patient in therapy will not continue treatment very long if he does not feel support from the therapist or from the group. In the moot the parties are encouraged in the expression of their complaints and feelings because they sense group support. The very presence of one's kinsmen and neighbors demonstrates their concern. It indicates to the parties that they have a real problem and that the others are willing to help them to help themselves in solving it. In a parallel vein, Frank, speaking of group psychotherapy, notes that: "Even anger may be supportive if it implies to a patient that others take him seriously enough to get angry at him, especially if the object of the anger feels it to be directed toward his neurotic behavior rather than himself as a person."[13] In the moot the feeling of support also grows out of the pronouncement of the blessings which stress the unity of the group and its harmonious goal, and it is also undoubtedly increased by the absence of the publicity and expressive symbols of political power which are found in the courtroom.

Permissiveness is the second element in therapy. It indicates to the patient that everyday restrictions on making anti-social statements or acting out anti-social impulses are lessened. Thus, in the Case of the Ousted Wife, Yua felt free enough to turn to her ousted co-wife (who had been married leviratically) and say:

> You don't respect me. You don't rely on me any more. When your husband was living, and I was with my husband, we slept on the farm. Did I ever refuse to send you what you

> asked me for when you sent a message? Didn't I always send you some of the meat my husband killed? Did I refuse to send you anything you wanted? When your husband died and we became co-wives, did I disrespect you? Why do you always make me ashamed? The things you have done to me make me sad.

Permissiveness in the therapeutic setting (and in the moot) results in catharsis, in a high degree of stimulation of feelings in the participants and an equally high tendency to verbalize these feelings.[14] Frank notes that: "Neurotic responses must be expressed in the therapeutic situation if they are to be changed by it."[15] In the same way, if the solution to a dispute reached in a house palaver is to be stable, it is important that there should be nothing left to embitter and undermine the decision. In a familiar setting, with familiar people, the parties to the moot feel at ease and free to say *all* that is on their minds. Yokpo, judged to be the wronged party in the Case of the Ousted Wife, in accepting an apology, gave expression to this when she said:

> I agree to everything that my people said, and I accept the things they have given me—I don't have *anything else* about them on my mind. *(My italics.)*

As we shall note below, this thorough airing of complaints also facilitates the gaining of insight into and the unlearning of idiosyncratic behaviour which is socially disruptive. Permissiveness is rooted in the lack of publicity and the lack of symbols of power. But it stems, too, from the immediacy of the hearing, the locus of investigatory initiative with the parties, and the wide range of relevance.

Permissiveness in therapy is impossible without the denial of reciprocity. This refers to the fact that the therapist will not respond in kind when the patient acts in a hostile manner or with inappropriate affection. It is a type of privileged indulgence which comes with being a patient. In the moot, the parties are treated in the same way and are allowed to hurl recriminations that, in the courtroom, might bring a few hours in jail as punishment for the equivalent of contempt of court. Even though inappropriate views are not responded to in kind, neither are they simply ignored. There is denial of *congruent* response, not denial of *any* response whatsoever. In the *bɛrɛi mu meni saa,* as in group psychotherapy; "private ideation and conceptualization are brought out into the open and all their facets or many of their facets exposed. The individual gets a "reading" from different bearings on the compass, so to speak,[16] and perceptual patterns . . . are joggled out of their fixed positions. . . ."[17]

Thus, Yua's outburst against Yokpo quoted above was not responded to with matching hostility, but its inappropriateness was clearly pointed out to her by the group. Some of them called her aside in a huddle and said to her:

> You are not right. If you don't like the woman, or she doesn't like you, don't be the first to say anything. Let her start and then say what you have to say. By speaking, if she heeds some of your words, the wives will scatter, and the blame will be on you. Then your husband will cry for your name that you have scattered his property.

In effect, Yua was being told that, in view of the previous testimony, her jealousy of her co-wife was not justified. In reality testing, she discovered that her view of the situation was not shared by the others and, hence was inappropriate. Noting how the others responded, she could see why her treatment of her co-wife had caused so much dissension. Her interpretation of her new co-wife's actions and resulting premises were not shared by the co-wife, nor by the others hearing a description of what had happened. Like psychotherapy, the moot is gently corrective of behavior rooted in such misunderstandings.

Similarly, Wama Nya, the husband, learned that others did not view as reasonable his accusing his wife of having a lover and urging her to go off and drink with the suspected paramour when he passed their house and wished them all a good evening. Reality testing for him taught him that the group did not view this type of mildly paranoid sarcasm as conducive to stable marital relationships.

The reaction of the moot to Yua's outburst indicates that permissiveness in this case was certainly not complete, but only relative, being much greater than in the courtroom. But without this moderated immunity the airing of grievances would be limited, and the chance for social relearning lessened. Permissiveness in the moot is incomplete because, even there, prudence is not thrown to the winds. Note that Yua was not told not to express her feelings at all, but to express them only after the co-wife had spoken so that, if the moot failed, she would not be in an untenable position In court there would be objection to her blunt speaking out. In the moot the objection was, in effect, to her speaking *out of turn*. In other cases the moot sometimes fails, foundering on this very point, because the parties are *too* prudent, all waiting for the others to make the first move in admitting fault.

The manipulation of rewards is the last dimension of therapy treated by Parsons. In this final phase of therapy[18] the patient is coaxed to conformity by the granting of rewards. In the moot one of the most important rewards is the group approval which goes to the wronged person who accepts an apology and to the person who is magnanimous enough to make one.

In the Case of the Ousted Wife, Kɔlɔ Waa, the mediator, and the others attending decided that the husband and the co-wife, Yua, had wronged Yokpo. Kɔlɔ Waa said to the husband:

> From now on, we don't want to hear of your fighting. You should live in peace with these women. If your wife accepts the things which the people have brought you should pay four chickens and ten bottles of rum as your contribution.

The husband's brother and sister also brought gifts of apology, although the moot did not explicitly hold them at fault.

By giving these prestations, the wrong-doer is restored to good grace and is once again acting like an "upright Kpelle" (although, if he wishes, he may refuse to accept the decision of the moot). He is eased into this position by being grouped with others to whom blame is also allocated, for, typically, he is not singled out and isolated in being labelled deviant. Thus, in the Case of the Ousted Wife, the children of Yokpo were held to be at fault in "being mean" to their stepfather, so that blame was not only shared by one "side," but ascribed to the other also.

Moreover, the prestations which the losing party is asked to hand over are not expensive. They are significant enough to touch the pocketbook a little; for the Kpelle say that if an apology does not cost something other than words, the wrong-doer is more likely to repeat the offending action. At the same time, as we noted above, the tokens are not so costly as to give the loser additional reason for anger directed at the other party which can undermine the decision.

All in all, the rewards for conformity to group expectations and for following out a new behaviour pattern are kept within the deviant's sight. These rewards are positive, in contrast to the negative sanctions of the courtroom. Besides the institutionalized apology, praise and acts of concern and affection replace fines and jail sentences. The mediator, speaking to Yokpo as the wronged party, said:

> You have found the best of the dispute. Your husband has wronged you. All the people have wronged you. You are the only one who can take care of them because you are the oldest. Accept the things they have given to you.

The moot in its procedural features and procedural sequences is, then, strongly analogous to psychotherapy. It is analogous to therapy in the structuring of the role of the mediator also. Parsons has indicated that, to do his job well, the therapist must be a member of two social systems: one containing himself and his patient; and the other, society at large.[19] He must not be seduced into thinking that he belongs only to the therapeutic dyad, but must gradually pull the deviant back into a relationship with the wider group. It is significant, then, that the mediator of a moot is a kinsman who is also a chief of some sort. He thus represents both the group involved in the dispute and the wider community. His task is to utilize his position as kinsman as a lever to manipulate the parties into living up to the normative requirements of the wider society, which, as chief, he upholds. His major orientation must be to the wider collectivity, not to the particular goals of his kinsmen.

When successful, the moot stops the process of alienation which drives two spouses so far apart that they are immune to ordinary social-control measures such as a smile, a frown, or a pointed aside.[20] A moot is not always successful, however. Both parties must have a genuine willingness to cooperate and a real concern about their discord. Each party must be willing to list his grievances, to admit his guilt, and make an open apology. The moot, like psychotherapy, is impotent without well-motivated clients.

The therapeutic elements found in the Kpelle moot are undoubtedly found in informal procedures for settling disputes in other African societies also; some of these are reported in literature and others are not. One such procedure which seems strikingly parallel to the Kpelle *bɛrɛi mu meni saa* has been described by J. H. M. Beattie.[21] This is the court of neighbors or *rukurato rw'enzarwa* found in the Banyoro kingdom of Uganda. The group also meets as an *ad hoc* assembly of neighbors to hear disputes involving kinsmen or neighbors.[22]

The intention of the Nyoro moot is to "reintegrate the delinquent into the community and, if possible, to achieve reconciliation without causing bitterness and resentment; in the words of an informant, the institution exists 'to finish off people's quarrels and to abolish bad feeling.'"[23] This therapeutic goal is manifested in the manner in which the dispute is resolved. After a decision is reached the penalty imposed is always the same. The party held to be in the wrong is asked to bring beer (four pots, modified downwards according to the circumstances) and meat, which is shared with the other party and all those attending the *rukurato.* The losing party is also expected to "humble himself, not only to the man he has injured but to the whole assembly."[24]

Beattie correctly points out that, because the council of neighbors has no power to enforce its decision, the shared feast is *not* to be viewed primarily as a penalty, for the wrong-doer acts as a host and also shares in the food and drink. "And it is a praiseworthy thing; from a dishonourable status he is promoted to an honourable one . . . "[25] and reintegrated into the community.[26]

Although Beattie does not use a psychoanalytic frame of reference in approaching his material, it is clear that the communal feast involves the manipulation of rewards as the last step in a social-control measure which breaks the progressive alienation of the deviance cycle. The description of procedures in the *rukurato* indicates that it is highly informal in nature, convening in a room in a house with everyone "sitting around." However, Beattie does not provide enough detail to enable one to determine whether or not the beginning and intermediate steps in the Nyoro moot show the permissiveness, support, and denial of reciprocity which characterize the Kpelle moot. Given the structure and outcome of most Nyoro councils, one would surmise that a close examination of their proceedings[27] would reveal the implicit operation of therapeutic principles.

The fact that the Kpelle court is basically coercive and the moot therapeutic does not imply that one is dysfunctional while the other is eufunctional. Like Beattie, I conclude that the court and informal dispute-settlement procedures have separate but complementary functions. In marital disputes the moot is oriented to a couple as a dyadic social system and serves to reconcile them wherever possible. This is eufunctional from the point of view of the couple, to whom divorce would be dysfunctional. Kpelle courts customarily treat matrimonial matters by granting a divorce. While this may be dysfunctional from the point of view of the couple, because it ends their marriage, it may be eufunctional from the point of view of society. Some marriages, if forced to continue, would result in adultery or physical violence at best, and improper socialization of children at worst. It is clear that the Kpelle moot is to the Kpelle court as the domestic and family relations courts (or commercial and labour arbitration boards) are to ordinary courts in our own society. The essential point is that both formal and informal dispute-settlement procedures serve significant functions in Kpelle society and neither can be fully understood if studied alone.[28]

NOTES

1. The field work on which this paper is based was carried out in Liberia in 1957 and 1958 and was supported by a grant from the Ford Foundation, which is, of course, not responsible for any of the views presented here. The data were analyzed while the writer was the holder of a pre-doctoral National Science Foundation Fellowship. The writer wishes to acknowledge, with gratitude, the support of both foundations. This paper was read at the Annual Meeting of the American Anthropological Association in Philadelphia, Pennsylvania, in November 1961.

   The dissertation, in which this material first appeared, was directed by Philip H. Gulliver, to whom I am indebted for much stimulating and provocative discussion of many of the ideas here. Helpful comments and suggestions have also been made by Robert T. Holt and Robert S. Merrill.

   Portions of the material included here were presented in a seminar on African Law conducted in the Department of Anthropology at the University of Minnesota by E. Adamson Hoebel and the writer. Members of the seminar were generous in their criticisms and comments.
2. Paul J. Bohannan, *Justice and Judgment among the Tiv,* Oxford University Press, London, 1957; Max Gluckman, *The Judicial Process among the Barotse of Northern Rhodesia,* Manchester University Press, 1954; P. P. Howell, *A Handbook of Nuer Law,* Oxford University Press, London, 1954.
3. Cf. George P. Murdock, *Social Structure,* Macmillan, New York, 1949, p. 74.
4. James L. Gibbs, Jr., "Poro Values and Courtroom Procedures in a Kpelle Chiefdom," *Southwestern Journal of Anthropology* (in press). A detailed analysis of Kpelle courtroom procedures and of procedures in the moot together with transcripts appears in: James L. Gibbs, Jr., *Some Judicial Implications of Marital Instability among the Kpelle* (unpublished Ph.D. Dissertation, Harvard University, Cambridge, Mass., 1960).
5. What follows is based on a detailed case study of moots in Panta Chiefdom and their contrast with courtroom hearings before the paramount chief of that chiefdom. Moots, being private, are less susceptible to the surveillance of the anthropologist than courtroom hearings, thus I have fewer transcripts of moots than of court cases. The analysis presented here is valid for Panta Chiefdom and also valid, I feel, for most of the Liberian Kpelle area, particularly the north-east where people are, by and large, traditional.
6. This simple distilled rum, bottled in Monrovia and retailing for twenty-five cents a bottle in 1958, is known in the Liberian Hinterland as "cane juice" and should not be confused with imported varieties.
7. American currency is the official currency of Liberia and is used throughout the country.
8. Cf. J. F. Holleman, "An Anthropological Approach to Bantu Law (with special reference to Shona law)" in the *Journal of the Rhodes-Livingstone Institute,* vol. x, 1950, pp. 27–41. Holleman feels that the use of tokens for effecting apologies—or marriages—shows the proclivity for reducing events of importance to something tangible.
9. Talcott Parsons, *The Social System,* The Free Press, Glencoe, Ill., 1951, pp. 314–19.
10. Jerome D. Frank, "Group Methods in Psychotherapy" in *Mental Health and Mental Disorder: A Sociological Approach,* edited by Arnold Rose, W. W. Norton Co., New York, pp. 524–35.
11. J. W. Klapman, Group Psychotherapy: Theory and Practice, Grune & Stratton, New York, 1959.
12. Marvin K. Opler, "Values in Group Psychotherapy," *International Journal of Social Psychiatry,* vol. iv, 1959, pp. 296–98.
13. Frank, op. cit., p. 531.
14. Ibid.
15. Ibid.
16. Klapman, op. cit., p. 39.
17. Ibid., p. 15.

18. For expository purposes the four elements of therapy are described as if they always occur serially. They may, and do, occur simultaneously also. Thus, all four of the factors may be implicit in a single short behavioural sequence. Parsons (op. cit.) holds that these four elements are common not only to psychotherapy but to all measures of social control.
19. Parsons, op. cit., p. 314. Cf. loc. cit., chap. 10.
20. Cf. Parsons, op. cit., chap. 7. Parsons notes that in any social-control action the aim is to avoid the process of alienation, that "vicious-cycle" phenomenon whereby each step taken to curb the non-conforming activity of the deviant has the effect of driving him further into his pattern of deviance. Rather, the need is to "reach" the deviant and bring him back to the point where he is susceptible to the usual everyday informal sanctions.
21. J. H. M. Beattie, "Informal Judicial Activity in Bunyoro," *Journal of African Administration,* vol. ix, 1957, pp. 188–95.
22. Disputes include matters such as a son seducing his father's wives, a grown son disobeying his father, or a husband or wife failing in his or her duties to a spouse. Disputes between unrelated persons involve matters like quarrelling, abuse, assault, false accusations, petty theft, adultery, and failure to settle debts. (Ibid., p. 190.)
23. Ibid., p. 194.
24. Beattie, op. cit., p. 194.
25. Ibid., p. 193.
26. Ibid., p. 195. Moreover, Beattie also recognizes the functional significance of the Nyoro moots, for he notes that: "It would be a serious error to represent them simply as clumsy, "amateur" expedients for punishing wrongdoers or settling civil disputes at an informal, sub official level." (Ibid.)
27. The type of examination of case materials that is required demands that field workers should not simply record cases that meet the "trouble case" criterion (cf. K. N. Llewellyn and E. A. Hoebel, *The Cheyenne Way,* Norman, Okla., University of Oklahoma Press, 1941; and E. A. Hoebel, *The Law of Primitive Man,* Cambridge, Mass., Harvard University Press, 1954), but that cases should be recorded in some transcript-like form.
28. The present study has attempted to add to our understanding of informal dispute-settlement procedures in one African society by using an eclectic but organized collection of concepts from jurisprudence, ethno-law, and psychology. It is based on the detailed and systematic analysis of a few selected cases, rather than a mass of quantitative data. In further research a greater variety of cases handled by Kpelle moots should be subjected to the same analysis to test its merit more fully.

DISCUSSION QUESTIONS

1. What types of cases are usually heard by moots? What types are heard by traditional courts?
2. How do the procedures of Kpelle moots differ from the procedures of traditional courts?
3. Gibbs says that the Kpelle moot tends to be more consensual than formal courts. In what specific ways are moots more consensual?

RESOURCES ON THE INTERNET

InfoTrac College Edition

(http://infotrac.thomsonlearning.com/index.html)

You can find further relevant readings by searching *InfoTrac College Edition,* an online library with access to thousands of scholarly and popular periodicals. Below are suggested search terms for this article:

- moot
- conflict resolution
- social control

Anthropology Online: Wadsworth's Anthropology Resource Center

(http://anthropology.wadsworth.com)

The Wadsworth Anthropology Resource Center contains a wealth of information and useful tools for students including information on careers in anthropology.

11

American Schoolrooms: Learning the Nightmare

JULES HENRY

Clifford Geertz, a former president of the American Anthropological Association, has claimed that a major role of cultural anthropology is to "keep the world off balance" by "pulling out rugs, upsetting tea tables, (and) setting off fire crackers." This is particularly true when the anthropological perspective of the outsider is turned on our own culture. In this selection, Jules Henry, by turning his anthropological lens upon his own society, is able to expose an appreciable gap between what we say we are doing in our educational institutions and what actually occurs. As North Americans, we like to think that our formal educational system both reflects and reinforces our values of individualism and competition by promoting free expression, creativity, and originality. But in a number of subtle ways our schools (through the actions of teachers, administrators, and peers) coerce students into conformity, causing them to acquiesce to the already existing societal norms. Thus, schools serve as mechanisms of social control, rather than liberating the mind and spirit.

School is an institution for drilling children in cultural orientations. Educators have attempted to free the school from drill, but have failed because they have always chosen the most obvious "enemy" to attack. Furthermore, with every enemy destroyed, new ones are installed among the old fortifications that are the enduring contradictory maze of the culture. Educators think that when they have made arithmetic or spelling into a game; made it unnecessary for children to "sit up straight"; defined the relation between teacher and children as democratic; and introduced plants, fish, and hamsters into schoolrooms, they have settled the problem of drill. They are mistaken.

The paradox of the human condition is expressed more in education than elsewhere in human culture, because learning to learn has been and continues to be *Homo sapiens'* most formidable evolutionary task. Although it is true that mammals, as compared to birds and fishes, have to learn so much that it is difficult to say by the time we get to chimpanzees which behavior is inborn and which is learned, the learning task has become so enormous for man that today, education, along with survival, constitutes a major preoccupation. In all the fighting over education we are simply saying that after a million years of struggling to become human, we are not yet satisfied that we have mastered the fundamental human task, learning.

Another learning problem inherent in the human condition is this: We must conserve culture while changing it, we must always be *more* sure of surviving than of adapting. Whenever a new idea appears, our first concern as *animals* must be that it does not kill us; then, and only then, can we look at it from other points of view. In general, primitive people solved this problem simply by walling their children off from new possibilities by educational methods that, largely through fear, so narrowed the perceptual sphere that nontraditional ways of viewing the world became unthinkable.

The function of education has never been to free the mind and the spirit of man, but to bind them. To the end that the mind and spirit of his children should never escape, *Homo sapiens* has wanted acquiescence, not originality, from his offspring. It is natural that this should be so, for where every man is unique there is no society, and where there is no society there can be no man. Contemporary American educators think they want creative children, yet it is an open question as to what they expect these children to create. If all through school the young were provoked to question the Ten Commandments, the sanctity of revealed religion, the foundations of patriotism, the profit motive, the two-party system, monogamy, the laws of incest, and so on, we would have more creativity than we could handle. In teaching our children to accept fundamentals of social relationships and religious beliefs without question we follow the ancient highways of the human race.

American classrooms, like educational institutions anywhere, express the values, preoccupations, and fears found in the culture as a whole. School has no choice; it must train the children to fit the culture as it is. School can give training in skills; it cannot teach creativity. Since the creativity that *is* encouraged—as in science and mathematics, for example—will always be that which satisfies the cultural drives at the time, all the American school can do is nurture that creativity when it appears.

Creative intellect is mysterious, devious, and irritating. An intellectually creative child may fail in social studies, for example, simply because he cannot understand the stupidities he is taught to believe as "fact." He may even end up agreeing with his teachers that he is "stupid" in social studies. He will not be encouraged to play among new social systems, values, and relationships, if for no other reason than that the social studies teachers will perceive such a child as a poor student. Furthermore, such a child will simply be unable to fathom the absurdities that seem transparent *truth* to the teacher. What idiot believes in the "law of supply and demand," for example? But the children who do, tend to *become* idiots; and learning to be an idiot is part of growing up! Or, as Camus put it, learning to be *absurd.* Thus the intellectually creative child who finds it impossible to learn to think the absurd the truth, who finds it difficult to accept absurdity as a way of life, usually comes to think himself stupid.

Schools have therefore never been places for the stimulation of young minds; they are the central conserving force of the culture, and if we observe them closely they will tell us much about the cultural pattern that binds us.

Much of what I am now going to say pivots on the inordinate capacity of a human being to learn more than one thing at a time. A child writing the word "August" on the board, for example, is not only learning the word "August," but also how to hold the chalk without making it squeak, how to write clearly, how to keep going even though the class is tittering at his slowness, how to appraise the glances of the children in order to know whether he is doing it right or wrong. If a classroom can be compared to a communications system—a flow of messages between teacher (transmitter) and pupils (receivers)—it is instructive to recall another characteristic of communications systems applicable to classrooms: their inherent tendency to generate *noise. Noise,* in communications theory, applies to all those random fluctuations of the system that cannot be controlled, the sounds that are not part of the message. The striking thing about the child is that along with his "messages about spelling" he learns all the noise in the system also. But—and mark this well—it is *not* primarily the message (the spelling) that constitutes the most important subject matter to be learned, but the noise! The most significant cultural learnings—primarily the cultural drives—are communicated as *noise.* Let us see the system operate in some of the contemporary suburban classrooms my students and I studied over a period of six years.

> It is March 17 and the children are singing songs from Ireland and her neighbors. The teacher plays on the piano, while the children sing. While some children sing, a number of them hunt in the index, find a song belonging to one of Ireland's neighbors, and raise their hands in order that they may be called on to name the next song. The singing is of that pitchless quality always heard in elementary school classrooms. The teacher sometimes sings through a song first, in her off-key, weakishly husky voice.

The usual reason for this kind of song period is that the children are "broadened" while they learn something about music and singing. But what the children in fact learn about singing is to sing like everybody else. (This phenomenon—the standard, elementary school pitchlessness of the English-speaking world—was impressive enough for D. H. Lawrence to mention it in *Lady Chatterley's Lover.* The difficulty in achieving true pitch is so pervasive among us that missionaries carry it with them to distant jungles, teaching the natives to sing hymns off key. Hence on Sundays we would hear our Pilagá Indian friends, all of them excellent musicians in the Pilagá scale, carefully copy the missionaries by singing Anglican hymns, translated into Pilagá, off key exactly as sharp or as flat as the missionaries sang.) Thus one of the first things a child with a good ear learns in elementary school is to be musically stupid; he learns to doubt or to scorn his innate musical capacities.

But possibly more important than this is the use to which teacher and pupils put the lesson in ways not related at all to singing or to Ireland and her neighbors. To the teacher this was an opportunity to let the children somehow share the social aspects of the lesson with her. The consequence was distraction from singing as the children hunted in the index, and the net result was to activate the children's drives toward competition, achievement, and dominance. In this way the song period was scarcely a lesson in singing, but rather one in extorting the maximal benefit for the Self from *any* situation.

The first lesson a child has to learn when he comes to school is that lessons are not what they seem. He must then forget this and act as if they were. This is the first step toward "school mental health"; it is also the first step in becoming absurd. The second lesson is to put the teachers' and students' criteria in place of his own. The child must learn that the proper way to sing is tunelessly and not the way he hears the music; that the proper way to paint is the way the teacher says, not the way he sees it; that the proper attitude is not pleasure, but competitive horror at the success of his classmates, and so on. And these lessons must be so internalized that he will fight his parents if they object. The early schooling process is not successful unless it has produced in the child an acquiescence in its criteria, unless the child *wants* to think the way school has taught him to think. What we see in kindergarten and the early years of school is the pathetic surrender of babies. How could it be otherwise?

Now nothing so saps self-confidence as alienation from the Self. It would follow that school, the chief agent in the process, must try to provide the children with "ego support," for culture tries to remedy the ills it creates. Hence the effort to give children recognition in our schools. Hence the conversion of the songfest into an exercise in Self-realization. That anything essential was nurtured in this way is an open question, for the kind of individuality that was recognized as the children picked titles out of the index was mechanical, without a creative dimension, and under the strict control of the teacher. In short, the school metamorphoses the child, giving it the kind of Self the school can manage, and then proceeds to minister to the Self it has made.

We can see this at work in another example:

> The observer is just entering her fifth-grade classroom for the observation period. The teacher says, "Which one of you nice, polite boys would like to take [the observer's] coat and hang it up?" From the waving hands, it would seem that all would like to claim the honor. The teacher chooses one child, who takes the observer's coat. . . . The teacher conducted the arithmetic lessons mostly by asking, "Who would like to tell the answer to the next problem?" This question was followed by the usual large and agitated forest of hands, with apparently much competition to answer.

What strike us here are the precision with which the teacher was able to mobilize the potentialities in the boys for the proper social behavior, and the speed with which they responded. The large number of waving hands proves that most of the boys have already become absurd; but they have no choice. Suppose they sat there frozen?

A skilled teacher sets up many situations in such a way that *a negative attitude can be construed only as treason*. The function of questions like, "Which one of you nice, polite boys would like to take [the observer's] coat and hang it up?" is to bind the children into absurdity—to compel them to acknowledge that absurdity is existence, to acknowledge that it is better to exist absurd than not to exist at all. The reader will have observed that the question is not put, "Who *has* the answer to the next problem?" but, "Who *would like to tell*" it? What at one time in our culture was phrased as a challenge to skill in arithmetic, becomes here an invitation to group participation. The essential issue is that *nothing is but what it is made to be by the alchemy of the system*.

In a society where competition for the basic cultural goods is a pivot of action, people cannot be taught to love one another. It thus becomes necessary for the school to teach children how to hate, and without appearing to do so, for our culture cannot tolerate the idea that babes should hate each other. How does the school accomplish this ambiguity? Obviously through fostering competition itself, as we can see in an incident from a fifth-grade arithmetic lesson.

> Boris had trouble reducing 12/16 to the lowest terms, and could only get as far as 6/8. The teacher asked him quietly if that was as far as he could reduce it. She suggested he "think." Much heaving up and down and waving of hands by the other children, all frantic to correct him. Boris pretty unhappy, probably mentally paralyzed. The teacher, quiet, patient, ignores the others and concentrates with look and voice on Boris. After a minute or two, she turns to the class and says, "Well, who can tell Boris what the number is?" A forest of hands appears, and the teacher calls Peggy. Peggy says that four may be divided into the numerator and the denominator.

Boris's failure has made it possible for Peggy to succeed; his misery is the occasion for her rejoicing. This is the standard condition of the contemporary American elementary school. To a Zuñi, Hopi, or Dakota Indian, Peggy's performance would seem cruel beyond belief, for competition, the wringing of success from somebody's failure, is a form of torture foreign to those noncompetitive cultures. Yet Peggy's action seems natural to us; and so it is. How else would you run our world?

Looked at from Boris's point of view, the nightmare at the blackboard was, perhaps, a lesson in controlling himself so that he would not fly shrieking from the room under enormous public pressure. Such experiences force every man reared in our culture, over and over again, night in, night out, even at the pinnacle of success, to dream not of success, but of failure. In school the external nightmare is internalized for life. Boris was not learning arithmetic only; he was learning the *essential nightmare also. To be successful in our culture one must learn to dream of failure.*

When we say that "culture teaches drives and values" we do not state the case quite precisely. We should say, rather, that culture (and especially the school) provides the occasions in which drives and values are *experienced in events* that strike us with *overwhelming and constant force.* To say that culture "teaches" puts the matter too mildly. Actually culture invades and infests the mind as an obsession. If it does not, it will be powerless to withstand the impact of critical differences, to fly in the face of contradiction, to so engulf the mind that the world is seen only as the culture decrees it shall be seen, to compel a person to be absurd. The central emotion in obsession is fear, and the central obsession in education is fear of failure. In school, one becomes absurd through being afraid; but paradoxically, *only by remaining absurd can one feel free from fear.*

Let us see how absurdity is reinforced: consider this spelling lesson in a fourth-grade class.

> The children are to play "spelling baseball," and they have lined up to be chosen for the two teams. There is much noise, but the teacher quiets it. She has selected a boy and a girl and sent them to the front of the room as team captains to choose their teams. As the boy and girl pick the children to form their teams, each child takes a seat in orderly succession around the room. Apparently they know the game well. Now Tom, who has not yet been chosen, tries to call attention to himself in order to be chosen. Dick shifts his position to be more in the direct line of vision of the choosers, so that he may not be overlooked. He seems quite anxious. Jane, Tom, Dick, and one girl whose name the observer does not know are the last to be chosen. The teacher even has to remind the choosers that Dick and Jane have not been chosen. . . .
>
> The teacher now gives out words for the children to spell, and they write them on the board. [Each word is a pitched ball, and each correctly spelled word is a base hit. The children move around the room from base to base as their teammates spell the words correctly.] The outs seem to increase in frequency as each side gets near the children chosen last. The children have great difficulty spelling "August." As they make mistakes, those in the seats say, "No!" The teacher says, "Man on third." As a child at the board stops and thinks, the teacher says, "There's a time limit; you can't take too long, honey." At last, after many children fail on "August" one child gets it right and returns, grinning with pleasure, to her seat. . . . The motivation level in this game seems terrific. All the children seem to watch the board, to know what's right and wrong, and seem quite keyed up. There is no lagging in moving from base to base. The child who is now writing "Thursday" stops to think after the first letter, and the children snicker. He stops after another letter. More snickers. He gets the word wrong. There are frequent signs of joy from the children when their side is right.

"Spelling baseball" is an effort to take the "weariness, the fever, and the fret" out of spelling by absurdly transforming it into a competitive game. Children are usually good competitors, though they may never become good spellers; and although they may never learn to *spell* success, they know what it *is,* how to go after it, and how it feels not to have it. A competitive game is indicated when children are failing, because the drive to succeed in the *game* may carry them to victory over the subject matter. But once a spelling lesson is cast in the form of a game of baseball a great variety of *noise* enters the system; because the sounds of *baseball* (the baseball "messages") cannot but be *noise* in a system intended to communicate *spelling.* If we reflect that one could not settle a baseball game by converting it into a spelling lesson, we see that baseball is bizarrely irrelevant to spelling. If we reflect further that a child who is a poor speller might yet be a magnificent ballplayer, we are even further impressed that learning spelling through baseball is learning by absurd association.

In making spelling into a baseball game one drags into the classroom whatever associations a child may have to the impersonal sorting process of kid baseball, but there are differences between the baseball world and the "spelling baseball" world also. One's failure is paraded before the class minute upon minute, until, when the worst spellers are the only ones left, the conspicuousness of the failures has been enormously increased. Thus the *noise* from baseball is amplified by a *noise* factor specific to the classroom.

It should not be imagined that I "object" to all of this, for in the first place I am aware of the indispensable social functions of the spelling game, and in the second place, I can see that the rendering of failure conspicuous cannot but intensify the quality of the essential nightmare, and thus render an important service to the culture. Without nightmares human culture has never been possible. Without hatred competition cannot take place except in games.

The unremitting effort by the system to bring the cultural drives to a fierce pitch must ultimately turn the children against one another; and though they cannot punch one another in the nose or pull one another's hair in class, they can vent some of their hostility in carping criticism of one another's work. Carping criticism, painfully evident in almost any American classroom, is viciously destructive of the early tillage of those creative impulses we say we cherish.

Listen to a fifth-grade class: The children are taking turns reading stories they have made up. Charlie's is called *The Unknown Guest.*

> "One dark, dreary night, on a hill a house stood. This house was forbidden territory for Bill and Joe, but they were going in anyway. The door creaked, squealed, slammed. A voice warned them to go home. They went upstairs. A stair cracked. They entered a room. A voice said they might as well stay and find out now; and their father came out. He laughed and they laughed, but they never forgot their adventure together."
>
> Teacher: Are there any words that give you the mood of the story?
>
> Lucy: He could have made the sentences a little better. . . .
>
> Teacher: Let's come back to Lucy's comment. What about his sentences?
>
> Gert: They were too short. [Charlie and Jeanne have a discussion about the position of the word "stood" in the first sentence.]
>
> Teacher: Wait a minute; some people are for getting their manners. . . .
>
> Jeff: About the room: the boys went up the stairs and one "cracked," then they were in the room. Did they fall through the stairs, or what?
>
> The teacher suggests Charlie make that a little clearer. . . .
>
> Teacher: We still haven't decided about the short sentences. Perhaps they make the story more spooky and mysterious.
>
> Gwynne: I wish he had read with more expression instead of all at one time.
>
> Rachel: Not enough expression.
>
> Teacher: Charlie, they want a little more expression from you. I guess we've given you enough suggestions for one time. [Charlie does not raise his head, which is bent over his desk as if studying a paper.] Charlie! I guess we've given you enough suggestions for one time, Charlie, haven't we?

If American children fail while one of their number succeeds, they carp. And why not? We must not let our own "inner Borises" befog our thinking. A competitive culture endures by tearing people down. Why blame the children for doing it?

The contemporary school is not all horrors; it has its gentler aspects as well. Nearing a conclusion, let us examine impulse release and affection as they appear in many suburban classrooms.

Impulse is the root of life, and its release in the right amount, time, and place is a primary concern of culture. Nowadays the problem of impulse release takes on a special character because of the epoch's commitment to "letting down the bars." This being the case, teachers have a task unique in the history of education: the fostering of impulse release rather than the installation of controls. Everywhere controls are breaking down, and firmness with impulse is no part of contemporary pedagogy of "the normal child." Rather, impulse release, phrased as "spontaneity," "life adjustment," "democracy," "permissiveness," and "mothering," has become a central doctrine of education. It persists despite tough-minded critics from the Eastern Seaboard who concentrate on curriculum. The teachers know better; the real, the persisting, subject matter is *noise*.

How can the teacher release children's emotions without unchaining chaos? How can she permit so much *noise* and not lose the message? Were they alive, the teachers I had in P.S. 10 and P.S. 186 in New York City, who insisted on absolute silence, would say that chaos does prevail in many modern classrooms and that the message *is* lost. But lest old-fashioned readers argue that the social structure has fallen apart, I will point out what does *not* happen: The children do not fight or wrestle, run around the room, throw things, sing loudly, or whistle. The boys do not attack the girls or vice versa. Children do not run in and out of the room. They do not make the teacher's life miserable. All this occurs when the social structure *is* torn down, but in the average suburban classrooms we studied, it never quite happens. Why not? Here are some excerpts from an interview with a second-grade teacher I'll call Mrs. Olan.

> In the one-room schoolhouse in which I first taught, the children came from calm homes. There was no worry about war, and there was no TV or radio. Children of today know more about what is going on; they are better informed. So you can't hold a strict rein on them.
>
> Children need to enjoy school and like it. They also need their work to be done; it's not all play. You must get them to accept responsibility and to do work on their own.

To the question, "What would you say is your own particular way of keeping order in the classroom?" Mrs. Olan says:

> Well, I would say I try to get that at the beginning of the year by getting this bond of affection and a relationship between the children and me. And we do that with stories; and I play games *with* them—don't just teach them how to play. It's what you get from living together comfortably. We have "share" times. . . . These are the things that contribute toward discipline. Another thing in discipline—it took me a long time to learn it, too: I thought I was the boss, but I learned that even with a child, if you speak to him as you would to a neighbor or a friend you get a better response than if you say, "Johnny, do this or that."

Mrs. Olan has a creed: Love is the path to discipline through permissiveness; and school is a continuation of family life, in which the values of sharing and democracy lead to comfortable living and ultimately to discipline. She continues:

> With primary children the teacher is a mother during the day; they have to be able to bring their problems to you. They get love and affection at home, and I see no reason not to give it in school.

To Mrs. Olan, mother of a 21-year-old son, second-grade children are pussy-cats. When asked, "Do you think the children tend to be quieter if the teacher is affectionate?" she says:

> If a teacher has a well-modulated voice and a pleasing disposition, her children are more relaxed and quiet. Children are like kittens: If kittens have a full stomach and lie in the sun they purr. If the atmosphere is such that the children are more comfortable, they are quiet. It is comfortable living that makes the quiet child. When you are shouting at them and they're shouting back at you, it isn't comfortable living.

It is clear to the observer that Mrs. Olan is no "boss," but lodges responsibility in the children. She clarifies the matter further:

> It means a great deal to them to give them their own direction. When problems do come up in the room we talk them over and discuss what is the right thing to do when this or that happens. Usually you get pretty good answers. They are a lot harder on themselves than I would be; so if any punishment comes along like not going to an assembly you have group pressure.

As the interviewer was leaving, Mrs. Olan remarked, "My children don't rate as high [on achievement tests] as other children. I don't push, and that's because I believe in comfortable living." *Noise* has indeed become subject matter.

In such classrooms the contemporary training for impulse release and fun is clear. There the children are not in uniform, but in the jerkins and gossamer of *The Midsummer Night's Dream;* it is a sweet drilling without pain. Since impulse and release and fun are a major requirement of the classroom, and since they must be contained within the four walls, the instrument of containment can only be affection. The teacher must therefore become a parent, for it is a parent above all who deals with the impulses of the child.

It is hard for us to see, since we consider most people inherently replaceable, that there is anything remarkable in a parent-figure like a teacher showering the symbols of affection on a child for a year and then letting him walk out of her life. However, this is almost unheard of outside the stream of Western civilization; and even in the West it is not common. As a matter of fact, the existence of *children* willing to accept such demonstrations is in itself an interesting phenomenon, based probably on the obsolescence of the two-parent family. (Today our children *do not have enough parents,* because parents are unable to do all that has to be done *by* parents nowadays.) The fact that a teacher can be demonstrative without inflicting deep wounds on *herself* implies a character structure having strong brakes on involvement. Her expressions of tenderness, then, must imply "so far and no farther"; and over the years, children must come to recognize this. If this were not so, children would have to be dragged shrieking from grade to grade and teachers would flee teaching, for the mutual attachment would be so deep that its annual severing would be too much for either to bear. And so this noise, too, teaches two lessons important to today's culture. From regular replacement-in-affection children learn that the affection-giving figure, the teacher, is replaceable also, and so they are drilled in uninvolvement. Meanwhile, they learn that the symbols of affectivity can be used ambiguously, and that they are not binding—that they can be scattered upon the world without commitment.

Again, the reader should not imagine that I am "against" affectionate classrooms. They are a necessary adjunct to contemporary childhood and to the socialization of parenthood (the "three-parent family") at this stage of our culture. Meanwhile, the dialectic of culture suggests that there is some probability that when love like this enters by the door, learning leaves by the transom.

What, then, is the central issue? The central issue is *love of knowledge* for its own sake, not as the creature of drive, exploited largely for survival and for prestige. Creative cultures have loved the "beautiful person"—meditative, intellectual, and exalted. As for the individual, the history of great civilizations reveals little except that creativity has had an obstinate way of emerging only in a few, and that it has never appeared in the mass of the people. Loving the beautiful person more, we may alter this.

The contemporary school is a place where children are drilled in very general cultural orientations, and where subject matter becomes to a very considerable extent the instrument for instilling them. Because school deals with masses of children, it can manage only by reducing children all to a common definition. Naturally that definition is determined by the cultural preoccupations and so school creates the *essential night-*

mare that drives people away from something (in our case, failure) and toward something (success). Today our children, instead of loving knowledge, become embroiled in the nightmare.

DISCUSSION QUESTIONS

1. What does Jules Henry mean when he says that students in the United States "learn the nightmare?"
2. Why is it, according to Henry, that schools have no choice but to train children to fit into their culture as it already exists?
3. This article by Henry was written in 1963. Are schools sufficiently different today that his thesis would be less valid for the twenty-first century?

RESOURCES ON THE INTERNET

InfoTrac College Edition

(http://infotrac.thomsonlearning.com/index.html)

You can find further relevant readings by searching *InfoTrac College Edition,* an online library with access to thousands of scholarly and popular periodicals. Below are suggested search terms for this article:

- educational system
- creativity

Anthropology Online: Wadsworth's Anthropology Resource Center

(http://anthropology.wadsworth.com)

The Wadsworth Anthropology Resource Center contains a wealth of information and useful tools for students including information on careers in anthropology.

12

The Notion of Witchcraft Explains Unfortunate Events

E. E. EVANS-PRITCHARD

Although the book from which this selection was drawn was published in 1937 (and based on fieldwork conducted in the 1920s), Evans-Pritchard's work on the meaning of witchcraft among the Azande of the Sudan is still relevant to modern anthropology. When most westerners hear the term witchcraft, *they associate it with a host of scary phenomena, including Halloween, the witch trials of colonial America, and high levels of psychological derangement on the part of both witches and the people who believe in their existence. For the Azande, however, there is nothing particularly frightening about witches, because witchcraft provides a perfectly rational system for explaining why events occur.*

To understand the Azande system of witchcraft as a system of explanation, we need only to acknowledge some mysterious powers of humans, not the supernatural powers of deities. In a very real sense, the use of witchcraft to explain unfortunate events is not appreciably different from any system of explanation that lacks absolute proof, such as a conspiracy theory of history or the belief in the power of prayer. Such a belief system, which westerners often dismiss as superstitious, childlike, and irrational, in no way contradicts what westerners would call natural, scientific, or empirical explanations for events. To illustrate, the Azande parents of a child that recently died of malaria would not deny that the immediate cause of death was the bite of an infected female anopheles mosquito. But these same parents would ask an additional question: "Why did the mosquito bite my child, when my neighbor's child was not bitten?" For the Azande parent, the answer to the question would seem obvious: our child was bewitched. And, as Evans-Pritchard shows in this piece, such an explanation would be no less reasonable than ascribing the child's death to "the will of God."

I

Witches, as the Azande conceive them, clearly cannot exist. None the less, the concept of witchcraft provides them with a natural philosophy by which the relations between men and unfortunate events are explained and a ready and stereotyped means of reacting to such events. Witchcraft beliefs also embrace a system of values which regulate human conduct.

From *Witchcraft, Oracles and Magic Among the Azandes* by E.E. Evans-Pritchard, pp. 18–32, 1937. Reprinted by permission of Oxford University Press.

Witchcraft is ubiquitous. It plays its part in every activity of Zande life; in agricultural, fishing, and hunting pursuits; in domestic life of homesteads as well as in communal life of district and court; it is an important theme of mental life in which it forms the background of a vast panorama of oracles and magic; its influence is plainly stamped on law and morals, etiquette and religion; it is prominent in technology and language; there is no niche or corner of Zande culture into which it does not twist itself. If blight seizes the ground-nut crop it is witchcraft; if the bush is vainly scoured for game it is witchcraft; if women laboriously bale water out of a pool and are rewarded by but a few small fish it is witchcraft; if termites do not rise when their swarming is due and a cold useless night is spent in waiting for their flight it is witchcraft; if a wife is sulky and unresponsive to her husband it is witchcraft; if a prince is cold and distant with his subject it is witchcraft; if a magical rite fails to achieve its purpose it is witchcraft; if, in fact, any failure or misfortune falls upon anyone at any time and in relation to any of the manifold activities of his life it may be due to witchcraft. The Zande attributes all these misfortunes to witchcraft unless there is strong evidence, and subsequent oracular confirmation, that sorcery or some other evil agent has been at work, or unless they are clearly to be attributed to incompetence, breach of a taboo, or failure to observe a moral rule.

To say that witchcraft has blighted the ground-nut crop, that witchcraft has scared away game, and that witchcraft has made so-and-so ill is equivalent to saying in terms of our own culture that the ground-nut crop has failed owing to blight, that game is scarce this season, and that so-and-so has caught influenza. Witchcraft participates in all misfortunes and is the idiom in which Azande speak about them and in which they explain them. To us witchcraft is something which haunted and disgusted our credulous forefathers. But the Zande expects to come across witchcraft at any time of the day or night. He would be just as surprised if he were not brought into daily contact with it as we would be if confronted by its appearance. To him there is nothing miraculous about it. It is expected that a man's hunting will be injured by witches, and he has at his disposal means of dealing with them. When misfortunes occur he does not become awestruck at the play of supernatural forces. He is not terrified at the presence of an occult enemy. He is, on the other hand, extremely annoyed. Someone, out of spite, has ruined his ground-nuts or spoilt his hunting or given his wife a chill, and surely this is cause for anger! He has done no one harm, so what right has anyone to interfere in his affairs? It is an impertinence, an insult, a dirty, offensive trick! It is the aggressiveness and not the eerieness of these actions which Azande emphasize when speaking of them, and it is anger and not awe which we observe in their response to them.

Witchcraft is not less anticipated than adultery. It is so intertwined with everyday happenings that it is part of a Zande's ordinary world. There is nothing remarkable about a witch—you may be one yourself, and certainly many of your closest neighbours are witches. Nor is there anything awe-inspiring about witchcraft. We do not become psychologically transformed when we hear that someone is ill—we expect people to be ill—and it is the same with Zande. They expect people to be ill, i.e. to be bewitched, and it is not a matter for surprise or wonderment.

I found it strange at first to live among Azande and listen to naïve explanations of misfortunes which, to our minds, have apparent causes, but after a while I learnt the idiom of their thought and applied notions of witchcraft as spontaneously as themselves in situations where the concept was relevant. A boy knocked his foot against a small stump of wood in the centre of a bush path, a frequent happening in Africa, and suffered pain and inconvenience in consequence. Owing to its position on his toe it was impossible to keep the cut free from dirt and it began to fester. He declared the witchcraft had made him knock his foot against the stump. I always argued with Azande and criticized their statements, and I did so on this occasion. I told the boy that he had knocked his foot against the stump of wood because he had been careless, and that witchcraft had not placed it in the path, for it had grown there naturally. He agreed that witchcraft had nothing to do with the stump of wood being in his path but added that he had kept his eyes open for stumps, as indeed every Zande does most carefully, and that if he had not been bewitched he would have seen the stump. As a conclusive argument for his view he remarked that all cuts do not take days to heal but, on the contrary, close quickly, for that is the nature of cuts. Why, then, had his sore festered and remained open if there were no witchcraft behind it? This, as I discovered before long, was to be regarded as the Zande explanation of sickness.

Shortly after my arrival in Zandeland we were passing through a government settlement and noticed that a hut had been burnt to the ground on the previous night. Its owner was overcome with grief as it had contained the beer he was preparing for a mortuary feast. He told us that he had gone the previous night to examine his beer. He had lit a handful of straw and raised it above his head so that light would be cast on the pots, and in so doing he had ignited the thatch. He, and my companions also, were convinced that the disaster was caused by witchcraft.

One of my chief informants, Kisanga, was a skilled wood-carver, one of the finest carvers in the whole kingdom of Gbudwe. Occasionally the bowls and stools which he carved split during the work, as one may well imagine in such a climate. Though the hardest woods be selected they sometimes split in process of carving or on completion of the utensil even if the craftsman is careful and well acquainted with the technical rules of his craft. When this happened to the bowls and stools of this particular craftsman he attributed the misfortune to witchcraft and used to harangue me about the spite and jealousy of his neighbours. When I used to reply that I thought he was mistaken and that people were well disposed towards him he used to hold the split bowl or stool towards me as concrete evidence of his assertions. If people were not bewitching his work, how would I account for that? Likewise a potter will attribute the cracking of his pots during firing to witchcraft. An experienced potter need have no fear that his pots will crack as a result of error. He selects the proper clay, kneads it thoroughly till he has extracted all grit and pebbles, and builds it up slowly and carefully. On the night before digging out his clay he abstains from sexual intercourse. So he would have nothing to fear. Yet pots sometimes break, even when they are the handiwork of expert potters, and this can only be accounted for by witchcraft. "It is broken—there is witchcraft," says the potter simply. . . .

II

In speaking to Azande about witchcraft and in observing their reactions to situations of misfortune it was obvious that they did not attempt to account for the existence of phenomena, or even the action of phenomena, by mystical causation alone. What they explained by witchcraft were the particular conditions in a chain of causation which related an individual to natural happenings in such a way that he sustained injury. The boy who knocked his foot against a stump of wood did not account for the stump by reference to witchcraft, nor did he suggest that whenever anybody knocks his foot against a stump it is necessarily due to witchcraft, nor yet again did he account for the cut by saying that it was caused by witchcraft, for he knew quite well that it was caused by the stump of wood. What he attributed to witchcraft was that on this particular occasion, when exercising his usual care, he struck his foot against a stump of wood, whereas on a hundred other occasions he did not do so, and that on this particular occasion the cut, which he expected to result from the knock, festered whereas he had had dozens of cuts which had not festered. Surely these peculiar conditions demand an explanation. Again, every year hundreds of Azande go and inspect their beer by night and they always take with them a handful of straw in order to illuminate the hut in which it is fermenting. Why then should this particular man on this single occasion have ignited the thatch of his hut? Again, my friend the wood-carver had made scores of bowls and stools without mishap and he knew all there was to know about the selection of wood, use of tools, and conditions of carving. His bowls and stools did not split like the products of craftsmen who were unskilled in their work, so why on rare occasions should his bowls and stools split when they did not split usually and when he had exercised all his usual knowledge and care? He knew the answer well enough and so, in his opinion, did his envious, back-biting neighbours. In the same way, a potter wants to know why his pots should break on an occasion when he uses the same material and technique as on other occasions; or rather he already knows, for the reason is known in advance, as it were. If the pots break it is due to witchcraft.

We shall give a false account of Zande philosophy if we say that they believe witchcraft to be the sole cause of phenomena. This proposition is not contained in Zande patterns of thought, which only assert that witchcraft brings a man into relation with events in such a way that he sustains injury.

In Zandeland sometimes an old granary collapses. There is nothing remarkable in this. Every Zande knows that termites eat the supports in course of time and that even the hardest woods decay after years of service. Now a granary is the summerhouse of a Zande homestead and people sit beneath it in the heat of the day and chat or play the African hole-game or work at some craft. Consequently it may happen that there are people sitting beneath the granary when it collapses and they are injured, for it is a heavy structure made of beams and clay and may be stored with eleusine as well. Now why should these particular people have been sitting under this particular granary at the particular moment when it collapsed? That it should collapse is easily intelligible, but why should it have collapsed at the particular moment when these particular people were sitting beneath it? Through years it might have collapsed, so why should it fall just when certain people sought its kindly shelter? We say that the granary collapsed because its supports were eaten away by termites; that is the cause that explains the collapse of the granary. We also say that people were sitting under it at the time because it was in the heat of the day and they thought that it would be a comfortable place to talk and work. This is the cause of people being under the granary at the time it collapsed. To our minds the only relationship between these two independently caused facts is their coincidence in time and space. We have no explanation of why the two chains of causation intersected at a certain time and in a certain place, for there is no interdependence between them.

Zande philosophy can supply the missing link. The Zande knows that the supports were undermined by termites and that people were sitting beneath the granary in order to escape the heat and glare of the sun. But he knows besides why these two events occurred at a precisely similar moment in time and space. It was due to the action of witchcraft. If there had been no witchcraft people would have been sitting under the granary and it would not have fallen on them, or it would have collapsed but the people would not have been sheltering under it at the time. Witchcraft explains the coincidence of these two happenings.

III

I hope I am not expected to point out that the Zande cannot analyse his doctrines as I have done for him. It is no use saying to a Zande "Now tell me what you Azande think about witchcraft" because the subject is too general and indeterminate, both too vague and too immense, to be described concisely. But it is possible to extract the principles of their thought from dozens of situations in which witchcraft is called upon to explain happenings and from dozens of other situations in which failure is attributed to some other cause. Their philosophy is explicit, but is not formally stated as a doctrine. A Zande would not say "I believe in natural causation but I do not think that that fully explains coincidences, and it seems to me that the theory of witchcraft offers a satisfactory explanation of them," but he expresses his thought in terms of actual and particular situations. He says "a buffalo charges," "a tree falls," "termites are not making their seasonal flight when they are expected to do so," and so on. Herein he is stating empirically ascertained facts. But he also says "a buffalo charged and wounded so-and-so," "a tree fell on so-and-so and killed him," "my termites refuse to make their flight in numbers worth collecting but other people are collecting theirs all right," and so on. He tells you that these things are due to witchcraft, saying in each instance, "So-and-so has been bewitched." The facts do not explain themselves or only partly explain themselves. They can only be explained fully if one takes witchcraft into consideration.

One can only obtain the full range of a Zande's ideas about causation by allowing him to fill in the gaps himself, otherwise one will be led astray by linguistic conventions. He tells you "So-and-so was bewitched and killed himself" or even simply that "So-and-so was killed by witchcraft." But he is telling you the ultimate cause of his death and not the secondary causes. You can ask him "How did he kill himself?" and he will tell you that he committed suicide by hanging himself from the branch of a tree. You can also ask "Why did he kill himself?" and he will tell you that it was because he was angry with his brothers. The cause of his death was hanging from a tree, and the cause of his hanging from a tree was his anger with his brothers. If you then ask a Zande why he should say that the man was bewitched if he committed suicide on account of his anger with his brothers, he will tell you that only crazy people commit suicide, and that if everyone who was angry with his brothers committed suicide there would soon be no people left in the world, and that if this man had not been bewitched he would not have done what he did do. If you persevere and ask why witchcraft caused the man to kill himself the Zande will reply that he supposes someone hated him, and if you ask him why someone hated him your informant will tell you that such is the nature of men.

For if Azande cannot enunciate a theory of causation in terms acceptable to us they describe happenings in an idiom that is explanatory. They are aware that it is particular circumstances of events in their relation to man, their harmfulness to a particular person, that constitutes evidence of witchcraft. Witchcraft explains *why* events are harmful to man and not *how* they happen. A Zande perceives how they happen just as we do. He does not see a witch charge a man, but an elephant. He does not see a witch push over a granary, but termites gnawing away its supports. He does not see a psychical flame igniting thatch, but an ordinary lighted bundle of straw. His perception of how events occur is as clear as our own.

IV

Zande belief in witchcraft in no way contradicts empirical knowledge of cause and effect. The world known to the senses is just as real to them as it is to us. We must not be deceived by their way of expressing causation and imagine that because they say a man was killed by witchcraft they entirely neglect the secondary causes that, as we judge them, were the true causes of his death. They are foreshortening the chain of events, and in a particular social situation are selecting the cause that is socially relevant and neglecting the rest. If a man is killed by a spear in war, or by a wild beast in hunting, or by the bite of a snake, or from sickness, witchcraft is the socially relevant cause, since it is the only one which allows intervention and determines social behaviour.

Belief in death from natural causes and belief in death from witchcraft are not mutually exclusive. On the contrary, they supplement one another, the one accounting for what the other does not account for. Besides, death is not only a natural fact but also a social fact. It is not simply that the heart ceases to beat and the lungs to pump air in an organism, but it is also the destruction of a member of a family and kin, of a community and tribe. Death leads to consultation of oracles, magic rites, and revenge. Among the causes of death witchcraft is the only one that has any significance for social behaviour. The attribution of misfortune to witchcraft does not exclude what we call its real causes but is superimposed on them and gives to social events their moral value.

Zande thought expresses the notion of natural and mystical causation quite clearly by using a hunting metaphor to define their relations. Azande always say of witchcraft that it is the *umbaga* or second spear. When Azande kill game there is a division of meat between the man who first speared the animal and the man who plunged a second spear into it. These two are considered to have killed the beast and the owner of the second spear is called the *umbaga*. Hence if a man is killed by an elephant Azande say that the elephant is the first spear and that witchcraft is the second spear and that together they killed the man. If a man spears another in war the slayer is the first spear and witchcraft is the second spear and together they killed him.

Since Azande recognize plurality of causes, and it is the social situation that indicates the relevant one, we can understand why the doctrine of witchcraft is not used to explain every failure and misfortune. It sometimes happens that the social situation demands a common-sense, and not a mystical, judgement of cause. Thus, if you tell a lie, or commit adultery, or steal, or deceive your prince, and are found out, you cannot elude punishment by saying that you were bewitched. Zande doctrine declares emphatically "Witchcraft does not make a person tell lies"; "Witchcraft does not make a person commit adultery"; "Witchcraft does not put adultery into a man. 'Witchcraft' is in yourself (you alone are responsible), that is, your penis becomes erect. It sees the hair of a man's wife and it rises and becomes erect because the only 'witchcraft' is, itself" ("witchcraft" is here used metaphorically); "Witchcraft does not make a person steal"; "Witchcraft does not make a person disloyal." Only on one occasion have I heard a Zande plead that he was bewitched when he had committed an offence and this was when he lied to me, and even on this occasion everybody present laughed at him and told him that witchcraft does not make people tell lies.

If a man murders another tribesman with knife or spear he is put to death. It is not necessary in such a case to seek a witch, for an objective towards which vengeance may be directed is already present. If, on the other hand, it is a member of another tribe who has speared a man his relatives, or his prince, will take steps to discover the witch responsible for the event.

It would be treason to say that a man put to death on the orders of his king for an offence against authority was killed by witchcraft. If a man were to consult the oracles to discover the witch responsible for the death of a relative who had been put to death at the orders of his king he would run the risk of being put to death himself. For here the social situation excludes the notion of witchcraft as on other occasions it pays no attention to natural agents and emphasizes only witchcraft. Also, if a man were killed in vengeance because the oracles said that he was a witch and had murdered another man with his witchcraft then his relatives could not say that he had been killed by witchcraft. Zande doctrine lays it down that he died at the hand of avengers because he was a homicide. If a man were to have expressed the view that his kinsman had been killed by witchcraft and to have acted upon his opinion by consulting the poison oracle, he might have been punished for ridiculing the king's poison oracle, for it was the poison oracle of the king that had given official confirmation of the man's guilt, and it was the king himself who had permitted vengeance to take its course.

In these situations witchcraft is irrelevant and, if not totally excluded, is not indicated as the principal factor in causation. As in our own society a scientific theory of causation, if not excluded, is deemed irrelevant in questions of moral and legal responsibility, so in Zande society the doctrine of witchcraft, if not excluded, is deemed irrelevant in the same situations. We accept scientific explanations of the causes of disease, and even of the causes of insanity, but we deny them in crime and sin because here they militate against law and morals which are axiomatic. The Zande accepts a mystical explanation of the causes of misfortune, sickness, and death, but he does not allow this explanation if it conflicts with social exigencies expressed in law and morals.

For witchcraft is not indicated as a cause for failure when a taboo has been broken. If a child becomes sick, and it is known that its father and mother have had sexual relations before it was weaned, the cause of death is already indicated by breach of a ritual prohibition and the question of witchcraft does not arise. If a man develops leprosy and there is a history of incest in his case then incest is the cause of leprosy and not witchcraft. In these cases, however, a curious situation arises because when the child or the leper dies it is necessary to avenge their deaths and the Zande sees no difficulty in explaining what appears to us to be most illogical behaviour. He does so on the same principles as when a man has been killed by a wild beast, and he invokes the same metaphor of "second spear." In the cases mentioned above there are really three causes of a person's death. There is the illness from which he dies, leprosy in the case of the man, perhaps some fever in the case of the child. These sicknesses are not in themselves products of witchcraft, for they exist in their own right just as a buffalo or a granary exist in their own right. Then there is the breach of a taboo, in the one case of weaning, in the other case of incest. The child, and the man, developed fever, and leprosy, because a taboo was broken. The breach of a taboo was the cause of their sickness, but the sickness would not have killed them it witchcraft had not also been operative. If witchcraft had not been present as "second spear" they would have developed fever and leprosy just the same, but they would not have died from them. In these instances there are two socially significant causes, breach of taboo and witchcraft, both of which are relative to different social processes, and each is emphasized by different people.

But where there has been a breach of taboo and death is not involved witchcraft will not be evoked as a cause of failure. If a man eats a forbidden food after he has made powerful punitive magic he may die, and in this case the cause of his death is known beforehand, since it is contained in the conditions of the situation in which he died even if witchcraft was also operative. But it does not follow that he will die. What does inevitably follow is that the medicine he has made will cease to operate against the person for whom it is intended and will have to be destroyed lest it turn against the magician who sent it forth. The failure of the medicine to achieve its purpose is due to breach of a taboo and not to witchcraft. If a man has had sexual relations with his wife and on the next day approaches the poison oracle it will not reveal the truth and its oracular efficacy will be permanently undermined. If he had not broken a taboo it would have been said that witchcraft had caused the oracle to lie, but the condition of the person who had attended the seance provides a reason for its failure to speak the truth without having to bring in the notion of witchcraft as an agent. No one will admit that he has broken a taboo before consulting the poison oracle, but when an oracle lies everyone is prepared to admit that a taboo may have been broken by someone.

Similarly, when a potter's creations break in firing witchcraft is not the only possible cause of the calamity. Inexperience and bad workmanship may also be reasons for failure, or the potter may himself have had sexual relations on the preceding night. The potter himself will attribute his failure to witchcraft, but others may not be of the same opinion.

Not even all deaths are invariably and unanimously attributed to witchcraft or to the breach of some taboo. The deaths of babies from certain diseases are attributed vaguely to the Supreme Being. Also, if a man falls suddenly and violently sick and dies, his relatives may be sure that a sorcerer has made magic against him and that it is not a witch who has killed him. A breach of the obligations of blood-brotherhood may sweep away whole groups of kin, and when one after another of brothers and cousins die it is the blood and not witchcraft to which their deaths are attributed by outsiders, though the relatives of the dead will seek to avenge them on witches. When a very old man dies unrelated people say that he has died of old age, but they do not say this in the presence of kinsmen, who declare that witchcraft is responsible for his death.

It is also thought that adultery may cause misfortune, though it is only one participating factor, and witchcraft is also believed to be present. Thus is it said that a man may be killed in warfare or in a hunting accident as a result of his wife's infidelities. Therefore, before going to war or on a large-scale hunting expedition a man might ask his wife to divulge the names of her lovers.

Even where breaches of law and morals do not occur witchcraft is not the only reason given for failure. Incompetence, laziness, and ignorance may be selected as causes. When a girl smashes her water-pot or a boy forgets to close the door of the hen-house at night they will be admonished severely by their parents for stupidity. The mistakes of children are due to carelessness or ignorance and they are taught to avoid them while they are still young. People do not say that they are effects of witchcraft, or if they are prepared to concede the possibility of witchcraft they consider stupidity the main cause. Moreover, the Zande is not so naïve that he holds witchcraft responsible for the cracking of a pot during firing if subsequent examination shows that a pebble was left in the clay, or for an animal escaping his net if someone frightened it away by a move or a sound. People do not blame witchcraft if a woman burns her porridge nor if she presents it undercooked to her husband. And when an inexperienced craftsman makes a stool which lacks polish or which splits, this is put down to his inexperience.

In all these cases the man who suffers the misfortune is likely to say that it is due to witchcraft, but others will not say so. We must bear in mind nevertheless that a serious misfortune, especially if it results in death, is normally attributed by everyone to the action of witchcraft, especially by the sufferer and his kin, however much it may have been due to a man's incompetence or absence of self-control. If a man falls into a fire and is seriously burnt, or falls into a game-pit and breaks his neck or his leg, it would undoubtedly be attributed to witchcraft. Thus when six or seven of the sons of Prince Rikita were entrapped in a ring of fire and burnt to death when hunting cane-rats their death was undoubtedly due to witchcraft.

Hence we see that witchcraft has its own logic, its own rules of thought, and that these do not exclude natural causation. Belief in witchcraft is quite consistent with human responsibility and a rational appreciation of nature. First of all a man must carry out an activity according to traditional rules of technique, which consist of knowledge checked by trial and error in each generation. It is only if he fails in spite of adherence to these rules that people will impute his lack of success to witchcraft.

V

It is often asked whether primitive peoples distinguish between the natural and the supernatural, and the query may be here answered in a preliminary manner in respect to the Azande. The question as it stands may mean, do primitive peoples distinguish between the natural and the supernatural in the abstract? We have a notion of an ordered world conforming to what we call natural laws, but some people in our society believe that mysterious things can happen which cannot be accounted for by reference to natural laws and which therefore are held to transcend them, and we call these happenings supernatural. To us supernatural means very much the same as abnormal or extraordinary. Azande certainly have no such notions of reality. They have no conceptions of "natural" as we understand it, and therefore neither of the "supernatural" as we understand it. Witchcraft is to Azande an ordinary and not an extraordinary, even though it may in some circumstances be an infrequent, event. It is a normal, and not an abnormal happening. But if they do not give to the natural and supernatural the meanings which educated Europeans give to them they nevertheless distinguish between them. For our question may be formulated, and should be formulated, in a different manner. We ought rather to ask whether primitive peoples perceive any difference between the happenings which we, the observers of their culture, class as natural and the happenings which we class as mystical. Azande undoubtedly perceive a difference between what we consider the workings of nature on the one hand and the workings of magic and ghosts and witchcraft on the other hand, though in the absence of a formulated doctrine of natural law they do not, and cannot, express the difference as we express it.

The Zande notion of witchcraft is incompatible with our ways of thought. But even to the Azande there is something peculiar about the action of witchcraft. Normally it can be perceived only in dreams. It is not an evident notion but transcends sensory experience. They do not profess to understand witchcraft entirely. They know that it exists and works evil, but they have to guess at the manner in which it works. Indeed, I have frequently been struck when discussing witchcraft with Azande by the doubt they express about the subject, not only in what they say, but even more in their manner of saying it, both of which contrast with their ready knowledge, fluently imparted, about social events and economic techniques. They feel out of their depth in trying to describe the way in which witchcraft accomplishes its ends. That it kills people is obvious, but how it kills them cannot be known precisely. They tell you that perhaps if you were to ask an older man or a witch-doctor he might give you more information. But the older men and the witch-doctors can tell you little more than youth and laymen. They only know what the others know: that the soul of witchcraft goes by night and devours the soul of its victim. Only witches themselves understand these matters fully. In truth Azande experience feelings about witchcraft rather than ideas, for their intellectual concepts of it are weak and they know better what to do when attacked by it than how to explain it. Their response is action and not analysis.

There is no elaborate and consistent representation of witchcraft that will account in detail for its workings, nor of nature which expounds its conformity to sequences and functional interrelations. The Zande actualizes these beliefs rather than intellectualizes them, and their tenets are expressed in socially controlled behaviour rather than in doctrines. Hence the difficulty of discussing the subject of witchcraft with Azande, for their ideas are imprisoned in action and cannot be cited to explain and justify action.

DISCUSSION QUESTIONS

1. What is the rationale for witchcraft in Azande society?
2. How does witchcraft function in Azande society? Can you think of any positive roles that witchcraft plays which contribute to the overall well-being of Azande society?
3. According to the Azande system of explanation, in what situations would witchcraft not be used to explain events?

RESOURCES ON THE INTERNET

InfoTrac College Edition

(http://infotrac.thomsonlearning.com/index.html)

You can find further relevant readings by searching *InfoTrac College Edition,* an online library with access to thousands of scholarly and popular periodicals. Below are suggested search terms for this article:

- witchcraft
- supernatural

Anthropology Online: Wadsworth's Anthropology Resource Center

(http://anthropology.wadsworth.com)

The Wadsworth Anthropology Resource Center contains a wealth of information and useful tools for students including information on careers in anthropology.

13

Baseball Magic

GEORGE GMELCH

Americans like to think of themselves as being grounded in scientific rationality rather than in superstition, magic, and ritual. Yet, when we turn the anthropological lens upon our own culture, we can see that magic and appeals to supernatural forces are employed in the United States for the very same reasons they are in the Trobriand Islands or among the Azande in the Southern Sudan—that is, to ensure success in human activities. Middle-class North Americans—and others—are likely to call on supernatural forces in those situations that are unpredictable and over which they have relatively little control.

In this article, George Gmelch, an anthropologist as well as a former professional baseball player, reminds us that U.S. baseball players are more likely to use magic (ritual, taboos, and fetishes) on those aspects of the game that are unpredictable (hitting and pitching) than on fielding, over which players have greater control. Even if this baseball magic doesn't always produce the desired outcome, it continues to be used because it functions to reduce anxiety and provide players with at least the illusion of control.

We find magic wherever the elements of chance and accident, and the emotional play between hope and fear have a wide and extensive range. We do not find magic wherever the pursuit is certain, reliable, and well under the control of rational methods.

—BRONISLAW MALINOWSKI

Professional baseball is a nearly perfect arena in which to test Malinowski's hypothesis about magic. The great anthropologist was not, of course, talking about sleight of hand but of rituals, taboos and fetishes that men resort to when they want to ensure that things go their own way. Baseball is rife with this sort of magic, but, as we shall see, the players use it in some aspects of the game far more than in others.

Everyone knows that there are three essentials of baseball—hitting, pitching and fielding. The point is, however, that the first two, hitting and pitching, involve a high degree of chance. The pitcher is the player least able to control the outcome of his own efforts. His best pitch may be hit for a bloop single while his worst pitch may be hit directly to one of his fielders for an out. He may limit the opposition to a single hit and lose, or he may give up a dozen hits and win. It is not uncommon for pitchers to perform well and lose, and vice versa; one has only to look at the frequency with which pitchers end a season with poor won-lost percentages but low earned run averages (number of runs given up per game). The opposite is equally true: some pitchers play poorly, giving up many runs, yet win many games. In

Reprinted by permission of Transaction Publishers. "Superstition and Ritual in American Baseball" by George Gmelch in *Society* 8(8): 39–41.

brief, the pitcher, regardless of how well he performs, is dependent upon the proficiency of his teammates, the inefficiency of the opposition and the supernatural (luck).

But luck, as we all know, comes in two forms, and many fans assume that the pitcher's tough losses (close games in which he gave up very few runs) are eventually balanced out by his "lucky" wins. This is untrue, as a comparison of pitchers' lifetime earned run averages to their overall won-lost records shows. If the player could apply a law of averages to individual performance, there would be much less concern about chance and uncertainty in baseball. Unfortunately, he cannot and does not.

Hitting, too, is a chancy affair. Obviously, skill is required in hitting the ball hard and on a line. Once the ball is hit, however, chance plays a large role in determining where it will go, into a waiting glove or whistling past a falling stab.

With respect to fielding, the player has almost complete control over the outcome. The average fielding percentage or success rate of .975 compared to a .245 success rate for hitters (the average batting average), reflects the degree of certainty in fielding. Next to the pitcher or hitter, the fielder has little to worry about when he knows that better than 9.7 times in ten he will execute his task flawlessly.

If Malinowski's hypothesis is correct, we should find magic associated with hitting and pitching, but none with fielding. Let us take the evidence by category—ritual, taboo and fetish.

RITUAL

After each pitch, ex-major leaguer Lou Skeins used to reach into his back pocket to touch a crucifix, straighten his cap and clutch his genitals. Detroit Tiger infielder Tim Maring wore the same clothes and put them on exactly in the same order each day during a batting streak. Baseball rituals are almost infinitely various. After all, the ballplayer can ritualize any activity he considers necessary for a successful performance, from the type of cereal he eats in the morning to the streets he drives home on.

Usually, rituals grow out of exceptionally good performances. When the player does well he cannot really attribute his success to skill alone. He plays with the same amount of skill one night when he gets four hits as the next night when he goes hitless. Through magic, such as ritual, the player seeks greater control over his performance, actually control over the elements of chance. The player, knowing that his ability is fairly constant, attributes the inconsistencies in his performance to some form of behavior or a particular food that he ate. When a player gets four hits in a game, especially "cheap" hits, he often believes that there must have been something he did, in addition to his ability, that shifted luck to his side. If he can attribute his good fortune to the glass of iced tea he drank before the game or the new shirt he wore to the ballpark, then by repeating the same behavior the following day he can hope to achieve similar results. (One expression of this belief is the myth that eating certain foods will give the ball "eyes," that is, a ball that seeks the gaps between fielders.) In hopes of maintaining a batting streak, I once ate fried chicken every day at 4:00 P.M., kept my eyes closed during the national anthem and changed sweat shirts at the end of the fourth inning each night for seven consecutive nights until the streak ended.

Fred Caviglia, Kansas City minor league pitcher, explained why he eats certain foods before each game: "Everything you do is important to winning. I never forget what I eat the day of a game or what I wear. If I pitch well and win I'll do it all exactly the same the next day I pitch. You'd be crazy not to. You just can't ever tell what's going to make the difference between winning and losing."

Rituals associated with hitting vary considerably in complexity from one player to the next, but they have several components in common. One of the most popular is tagging a particular base when leaving and returning to the dugout each inning. Tagging second base on the way to the outfield is habitual with some players. One informant reported that during a successful month of the season he stepped on third base on his way to the dugout after the third, sixth and ninth innings of each game. Asked if he ever purposely failed to step on the bag he replied, "Never! I wouldn't dare, it would destroy my confidence to hit." It is not uncommon for a hitter who is playing poorly to try different combinations of tagging and not tagging particular bases in an attempt to find a successful combination. Other components of a hitter's ritual may include tapping the plate with his bat a precise number of times or taking a precise number of warm-up swings with the leaded bat.

One informant described a variation of this in which he gambled for a certain hit by tapping the plate a fixed number of times. He touched the plate once with his bat for each base desired: one tap for a single, two for a double and so on. He even built in odds that prevented him from asking for a home run each time. The odds of hitting a single with one tap were one in three, while the chances of hitting a home run with four taps were one in 12.

Clothing is often considered crucial to both hitters and pitchers. They may have several athletic supporters and a number of sweat shirts with ritual significance. Nearly all players wear the same uniform and undergarments each day when playing well, and some even wear the same street clothes. In 1954, the New York Giants, during a 16-game winning streak, wore the same clothes in each game and refused to let them be cleaned for fear that their good fortune might be washed away with the dirt. The route taken to and from the stadium can also have significance some players drive the same streets to the ballpark during a hitting streak and try different routes during slumps.

Because pitchers only play once every four days, the rituals they practice are often more complex than the hitters', and most of it, such as tugging the cap between pitches, touching the rosin bag after each bad pitch or smoothing the dirt on the mound before each new batter, takes place on the field. Many baseball fans have observed this behavior never realizing that it may be as important to the pitcher as throwing the ball.

Dennis Grossini, former Detroit farmhand, practiced the following ritual on each pitching day for the first three months of a winning season. First, he arose from bed at exactly 10:00 A.M. and not a minute earlier or later. At 1:00 P.M. he went to the nearest restaurant for two glasses of iced tea and a tuna fish sandwich. Although the afternoon was free, he observed a number of taboos such as no movies, no reading and no candy. In the clubhouse he changed into the sweat shirt and jock he wore during his last winning game, and one hour before the game he chewed a wad of Beechnut chewing tobacco. During the game he touched his letters (the team name on his uniform) after each pitch and straightened his cap after each ball. Before the start of each inning he replaced the pitcher's rosin bag next to the spot where it was the inning before. And after every inning in which he gave up a run he went to the clubhouse to wash his hands. I asked him which part of the ritual was most important. He responded: "You can't really tell what's most important so it all becomes important. I'd be afraid to change anything. As long as I'm winning I do everything the same. Even when I can't wash my hands [this would occur when he must bat] it scares me going back to the mound. . . . I don't feel quite right."

One ritual, unlike those already mentioned, is practiced to improve the power of the baseball bat. It involves sanding the bat until all the varnish is removed, a process requiring several hours of labor, then rubbing rosin into the grain of the bat before finally heating it over a flame. This ritual treatment supposedly increases the distance the ball travels after being struck. Although some North Americans prepare their bats in this fashion it is more popular among Latin Americans. One informant admitted that he was not certain of the effectiveness of the treatment. But, he added, "There may not be a God, but I go to church just the same."

Despite the wide assortment of rituals associated with pitching and hitting, I never observed any ritual related to fielding. In all my 20 interviews only one player, a shortstop with acute fielding problems, reported any ritual even remotely connected to fielding.

TABOO

Mentioning that a no-hitter is in progress and crossing baseball bats are the two most widely observed taboos. It is believed that if the pitcher hears the words "no-hitter" his spell will be broken and the no-hitter lost. As for the crossing of bats, that is sure to bring bad luck; batters are therefore extremely careful not to drop their bats on top of another. Some players elaborate this taboo even further. On one occasion a teammate became quite upset when another player tossed a bat from the batting cage and it came to rest on top of his. Later he explained that the top bat would steal hits from the lower one. For him, then, bats contain a finite number of hits, a kind of baseball "image of limited good." Honus Wagner, a member of baseball's Hall of Fame, believed that each bat was good for only 100 hits and no more. Regardless of the quality of the bat he would discard it after its 100th hit.

Besides observing the traditional taboos just mentioned, players also observe certain personal prohibitions. Personal taboos grow out of exceptionally poor performances, which a player often attributes to some particular behavior or food. During my first season of professional baseball I once ate pancakes before a game in which I struck out four times. Several weeks later I had a repeat performance, again after eating pancakes. The result was a pancake taboo in which from that day on I never ate pancakes during the season. Another personal taboo, born out of similar circumstances, was against holding a baseball during the national anthem.

Taboos are also of many kinds. One athlete was careful never to step on the chalk foul lines or the chalk lines of the batter's box. Another would never put on his cap until the game started and would not wear it at all on the days he did not pitch. Another had a movie taboo in which he refused to watch a movie the day of a game. Often certain uniform numbers become taboo. If a player has a poor spring training or a bad year, he may refuse to wear the same uniform number again. I would not wear double numbers, especially 44 and 22. On several occasions, teammates who were playing poorly requested a change of uniform during the middle of the season. Some players consider it so important that they will wear the wrong size uniform just to avoid a certain number or to obtain a good number.

Again, with respect to fielding, I never saw or heard of any taboos being observed, though of course there were some taboos, like the uniform numbers, that were concerned with overall performance and so included fielding.

FETISHES

These are standard equipment for many baseball players. They include a wide assortment of objects: horsehide covers of old baseballs, coins, bobby pins, protective cups, crucifixes and old bats. Ordinary objects are given this power in a fashion similar to the formation of taboos and rituals. The player during an exceptionally hot batting or pitching streak, especially one in which he has "gotten all the breaks," credits some unusual object, often a new possession, for his good fortune. For example, a player in a slump might find a coin or an odd stone just before he begins a hitting streak. Attributing the improvement in his performance to the new object, it becomes a fetish, embodied with supernatural power. While playing for Spokane, Dodger pitcher Alan Foster forgot his baseball shoes on a road trip and borrowed a pair from a teammate to pitch. That night he pitched a no-hitter and later, needless to say, bought the shoes from his teammate. They became his most prized possession.

Fetishes are taken so seriously by some players that their teammates will not touch them out of fear of offending the owner. I once saw a fight caused by the desecration of a fetish. Before the game, one player stole the fetish, a horsehide baseball cover, out of a teammate's back pocket. The prankster did not return the fetish until after the game, in which the owner of the fetish went hitless, breaking a batting streak. The owner, blaming his inability to hit on the loss of the fetish, lashed out at the thief when the latter tried to return it.

Rube Waddel, an old-time Philadelphia Athletic pitching great, had a hairpin fetish. However, the hairpin he possessed was only powerful as long as he won. Once he lost a game he would look for another hairpin, which had to be found on the street, and he would not pitch until he found another.

The use of fetishes follows the same pattern as ritual and taboo in that they are connected only with hitting or pitching. In nearly all cases the player expressed a specific purpose for carrying a fetish, but never did a player perceive his fetish as having any effect on his fielding.

I have said enough, I think, to show that many of the beliefs and practices of professional baseball players are magical. Any empirical connection between the ritual taboo and fetishes and the desired event is quite absent. Indeed, in several instances the relationship between the cause and effect, such as eating tuna fish sandwiches to win a ball game, is even more remote than is characteristic of primitive magic. Note, however, that unlike many forms of primitive magic, baseball magic is usually performed to achieve one's own end and not to block someone else's. Hitters do not tap their bats on the plate to hex the pitcher but to improve their own performance.

Finally, it should be plain that nearly all the magical practices that I participated in, observed or elicited, support Malinowski's hypothesis that magic appears in situations of chance and uncertainty. The large amount of uncertainty in pitching and hitting best explains the elaborate magical practices used for these activities. Conversely, the high success rate in fielding, .975, involving much less uncertainty offers the best explanation for the absence of magic in this realm.

DISCUSSION QUESTIONS

1. How would you distinguish among a ritual, a taboo, and a fetish?
2. Of the three aspects of the game of baseball (fielding, hitting, and pitching), which are the most susceptible to baseball magic?
3. Can you think of how magic is used in other American sports?

RESOURCES ON THE INTERNET

InfoTrac College Edition

(http://infotrac.thomsonlearning.com/index.html)

You can find further relevant readings by searching *InfoTrac College Edition,* an online library with access to thousands of scholarly and popular periodicals. Below are suggested search terms for this article:

- magic
- taboo
- fetish

Anthropology Online: Wadsworth's Anthropology Resource Center

(http://anthropology.wadsworth.com)

The Wadsworth Anthropology Resource Center contains a wealth of information and useful tools for students including information on careers in anthropology.

14

Steel Axes for Stone-Age Australians

LAURISTON SHARP

For decades, anthropologists have recognized that cultures are more than the sum of their parts (things, ideas, and behavior patterns). Rather, cultures are integrated wholes, the parts of which are integrated. This means, of course, that a change in one part of a culture is likely to bring about changes in other parts of the culture. In this classic selection on the aboriginal Yir Yoront of Australia, Lauriston Sharp shows how the introduction of steel axes to Yir Yoront culture in the 1930s by well-meaning but shortsighted missionaries changed the relationship among family members and trading partners and eventually contributed to the demise of the culture.

This general principle of integrated cultures—so dramatically illustrated by Sharp—has important implications for anyone today working with people from other cultures, such as Peace Corps volunteers, foreign aid personnel, or international businesspeople. To illustrate, the introduction of a seemingly harmless commercial product or agricultural development program could have profoundly disruptive effects on the very fabric of the local culture. By knowing how the various parts of a culture are interconnected ahead of time, *the humane and responsible foreign aid worker or global businessperson will be able to predict possible harmful effects of introducing changes into other cultures.*

I

Like other Australian aboriginals, the Yir Yoront group which lives at the mouth of the Coleman River on the west coast of Cape York Peninsula originally had no knowledge of metals. Technologically their culture was of the old stone age or paleolithic type. They supported themselves by hunting and fishing, and obtained vegetables and other materials from the bush by simple gathering techniques. Their only domesticated animal was the dog; they had no cultivated plants of any kind. Unlike some other aboriginal groups, however, the Yir Yoront did have polished stone axes hafted in short handles which were most important in their economy.

Towards the end of the 19th century metal tools and other European artifacts began to filter into the Yir Yoront territory. The flow increased with the gradual expansion of the white frontier

From "Steel Axes for Stone-Age Australians" in *Human Organization*, Summer 1952, pp. 17–22. Reprinted with permission from the Society for Applied Anthropology.

outward from southern and eastern Queensland. Of all the items of western technology thus made available, the hatchet, or short handled steel axe, was the most acceptable to and the most highly valued by all aboriginals.

In the mid 1930's an American anthropologist lived alone in the bush among the Yir Yoront for 13 months without seeing another white man. The Yir Yoront were thus still relatively isolated and continued to live an essentially independent economic existence, supporting themselves entirely by means of their old stone age techniques. Yet their polished stone axes were disappearing fast and being replaced by steel axes which came to them in considerable numbers, directly or indirectly, from various European sources to the south.

What changes in the life of the Yir Yoront still living under aboriginal conditions in the Australian bush could be expected as a result of their increasing possession and use of the steel axe?

II

THE COURSE OF EVENTS

Events leading up to the introduction of the steel axe among the Yir Yoront begin with the advent of the second known group of Europeans to reach the shores of the Australian continent. In 1623 a Dutch expedition landed on the coast where the Yir Yoront now live.[1] In 1935 the Yir Yoront were still using the few cultural items recorded in the Dutch log for the aboriginals they encountered. To this cultural inventory the Dutch added beads and pieces of iron which they offered in an effort to attract the frightened "Indians." Among these natives metal and beads have disappeared, together with any memory of this first encounter with whites.

The next recorded contact in this area was in 1864. Here there is more positive assurance that the natives concerned were the immediate ancestors of the Yir Yoront community. These aboriginals had the temerity to attack a party of cattle men who were driving a small herd from southern Queensland through the length of the then unknown Cape York Peninsula to a newly established government station at the northern tip.[2] Known as the "Battle of the Mitchell River," this was one of the rare instances in which Australian aboriginals stood up to European gunfire for any length of time. A diary kept by the cattle men records that: ". . . 10 carbines poured volley after volley into them from all directions, killing and wounding with every shot with very little return, nearly all their spears having already been expended. . . . About 30 being killed, the leader thought it prudent to hold his hand, and let the rest escape. Many more must have been wounded and probably drowned, for 59 rounds were counted as discharged." The European party was in the Yir Yoront area for three days; they then disappeared over the horizon to the north and never returned. In the almost three-year long anthropological investigation conducted some 70 years later—in all the material of hundreds of free association interviews, in texts of hundreds of dreams and myths, in genealogies, and eventually in hundreds of answers to direct and indirect questioning on just this particular matter—there was nothing that could be interpreted as a reference to this shocking contact with Europeans.

The aboriginal accounts of their first remembered contact with whites begin in about 1900 with references to persons known to have had sporadic but lethal encounters with them. From that time on whites continued to remain on the southern periphery of Yir Yoront territory. With the establishment of cattle stations (ranches) to the south, cattle men made occasional excursions among the "wild black-fellows" in order to inspect the country and abduct natives to be trained as cattle boys and "house girls." At least one such

1. An account of this expedition from Amboina is given in R. Logan Jack, *Northmost Australia* (2 vols.), London, 1921, Vol. 1, pp. 18–57.

2. R. Logan Jack, *op. cit.*, pp. 298–335.

expedition reached the Coleman River where a number of Yir Yoront men and women were shot for no apparent reason.

About this time the government was persuaded to sponsor the establishment of three mission stations along the 700-mile western coast of the Peninsula in an attempt to help regulate the treatment of natives. To further this purpose a strip of coastal territory was set aside as an aboriginal reserve and closed to further white settlement.

In 1915, an Anglican mission station was established near the mouth of the Mitchell River, about a three-day march from the heart of the Yir Yoront country. Some Yir Yoront refused to have anything to do with the mission, others visited it occasionally, while only a few eventually settled more or less permanently in one of the three "villages" established at the mission.

Thus the majority of the Yir Yoront continued to live their old self-supporting life in the bush, protected until 1942 by the government reserve and the intervening mission from the cruder realities of the encroaching new order from the south. To the east was poor, uninhabited country. To the north were other bush tribes extending on along the coast to the distant Archer River Presbyterian mission with which the Yir Yoront had no contact. Westward was the shallow Gulf of Carpentaria on which the natives saw only a mission lugger making its infrequent dry season trips to the Mitchell River. In this protected environment for over a generation the Yir Yoront were able to recuperate from shocks received at the hands of civilized society. During the 1930's their raiding and fighting, their trading and stealing of women, their evisceration and two- or three-year care of their dead, and their totemic ceremonies continued, apparently uninhibited by western influence. In 1931 they killed a European who wandered into their territory from the east, but the investigating police never approached the group whose members were responsible for the act.

As a direct result of the work of the Mitchell River mission, all Yir Yoront received a great many more western artifacts of all kinds than ever before. As part of their plan for raising native living standards, the missionaries made it possible for aboriginals living at the mission to earn some western goods, many of which were then given or traded to natives still living under bush conditions; they also handed out certain useful articles gratis to both mission and bush aboriginals. They prevented guns, liquor, and damaging narcotics, as well as decimating diseases, from reaching the tribes of this area, while encouraging the introduction of goods they considered "improving." As has been noted, no item of western technology available, with the possible exception of trade tobacco, was in greater demand among all groups of aboriginals than the short handled steel axe. The mission always kept a good supply of these axes in stock; at Christmas parties or other mission festivals they were given away to mission or visiting aboriginals indiscriminately and in considerable numbers. In addition, some steel axes as well as other European goods were still traded in to the Yir Yoront by natives in contact with cattle stations in the south. Indeed, steel axes had probably come to the Yir Yoront through established lines of aboriginal trade long before any regular contact with whites had occurred.

III
RELEVANT FACTORS

If we concentrate our attention on Yir Yoront behavior centering about the original stone axe (rather than on the axe—the object—itself) as a cultural trait or item of cultural equipment, we should get some conception of the role this implement played in aboriginal culture. This, in turn, should enable us to foresee with considerable accuracy some of the results stemming from the displacement of the stone axe by the steel axe.

The production of a stone axe required a number of simple technological skills. With the various details of the axe well in mind, adult men could set about producing it (a task not considered appropriate for women or children). First of all a man had to know the location and properties of several natural resources found in his immediate environment: pliable wood for a handle, which could be doubled or bent over the axe head and bound tightly; bark, which could be rolled into cord for the binding; and gum, to fix the stone head in the haft. These materials had to be correctly gathered, stored, prepared, cut to size and applied or manipulated. They were in plentiful supply, and could be taken from anyone's property without special permission. Postponing consideration of the stone head, the axe could be made by any normal man who had a simple knowledge of nature and of the technological skills involved, together with fire (for heating the gum), and a few simple cutting tools—perhaps the sharp shells of plentiful bivalves.

The use of the stone axe as a piece of capital equipment used in producing other goods indicates its very great importance to the subsistence economy of the aboriginal. Anyone—man, woman, or child—could use the axe; indeed, it was used primarily by women, for theirs was the task of obtaining sufficient wood to keep the family campfire burning all day, for cooking or other purposes, and all night against mosquitoes and cold (for in July, winter temperature might drop below 40 degrees). In a normal lifetime a woman would use the axe to cut or knock down literally tons of firewood. The axe was also used to make other tools or weapons, and a variety of material equipment required by the aboriginal in his daily life. The stone axe was essential in the construction of the wet season domed huts which keep out some rain and some insects; of platforms which provide dry storage; of shelters which give shade in the dry summer when days are bright and hot. In hunting and fishing and in gathering vegetable or animal food the axe was also a necessary tool, and in this tropical culture, where preservatives or other means of storage are lacking, the natives spend more time obtaining food than in any other occupation—except sleeping. In only two instances was the use of the stone axe strictly limited to adult men: for gathering wild honey, the most prized food known to the Yir Yoront; and for making the secret paraphernalia for ceremonies. From this brief listing of some of the activities involving the use of the axe, it is easy to understand why there was at least one stone axe in every camp, in every hunting or fighting party, and in every group out on a "walk-about" in the bush.

The stone axe was also prominent in interpersonal relations. Yir Yoront men were dependent upon interpersonal relations for their stone axe heads, since the flat, geologically-recent, alluvial country over which they range provides no suitable stone for this purpose. The stone they used came from quarries 400 miles to the south, reaching the Yir Yoront through long lines of male trading partners. Some of these chains terminated with the Yir Yoront men, others extended on farther north to other groups, using Yir Yoront men as links. Almost every older adult man had one or more regular trading partners, some to the north and some to the south. He provided his partner or partners in the south with surplus spears, particularly fighting spears tipped with the barbed spines of sting ray which snap into viscious fragments when they penetrate human flesh. For a dozen such spears, some of which he may have obtained from a partner to the north, he would receive one stone axe head. Studies have shown that the sting ray barb spears increased in value as they move south and farther from the sea. One hundred and fifty miles south of Yir Yoront one such spear may be exchanged for one stone axe head. Although actual investigations could not be made, it was presumed that farther south, nearer the quarries, one sting ray barb spear would bring several stone axe heads. Apparently people who acted as links in the middle of the chain and who made neither spears nor axe heads would receive a certain number of each as a middleman's profit.

Thus trading relations, which may extend the individual's personal relationships beyond that of his own group, were associated with spears and axes, two of the most important items in a man's equipment. Finally, most of the exchanges took place during the dry season, at the time of the great aboriginal celebrations centering about initiation rites or other totemic ceremonials which attracted hundreds and were the occasion for much exciting activity in addition to trading.

Returning to the Yir Yoront, we find that adult men kept their axes in camp with their other equipment, or carried them when travelling. Thus a woman or child who wanted to use an axe—as might frequently happen during the day—had to get one from a man, use it promptly, and return it in good condition. While a man might speak of "my axe," a woman or child could not.

This necessary and constant borrowing of axes from older men by women and children was in accordance with regular patterns of kinship behavior. A woman would expect to use her husband's axe unless he himself was using it; if unmarried, or if her husband was absent, a woman would go first to her older brother or to her father. Only in extraordinary circumstances would she seek a stone axe from other male kin. A girl, a boy, or a young man would look to a father or an older brother to provide an axe for their use. Older men, too, would follow similar rules if they had to borrow an axe.

It will be noted that all of these social relationships in which the stone axe had a place are pair relationships and that the use of the axe helped to define and maintain their character and the roles of the two individual participants. Every active relationship among the Yir Yoront involved a definite and accepted status of superordination or subordination. A person could have no dealings with another on exactly equal terms. The nearest approach to equality was between brothers, although the older was always superordinate to the younger. Since the exchange of goods in a trading relationship involved a mutual reciprocity, trading partners usually stood in a brotherly type of relationship, although one was always classified as older than the other and would have some advantage in case of dispute. It can be seen that repeated and widespread conduct centering around the use of the axe helped to generalize and standardize these sex, age, and kinship roles both in their normal benevolent and exceptional malevolent aspects.

The status of any individual Yir Yoront was determined not only by sex, age, and extended kin relationships, but also by membership in one of two dozen patrilineal totemic clans into which the entire community was divided.[3] Each clan had literally hundreds of totems, from one or two of which the clan derived its name, and the clan members their personal names. These totems included natural species or phenomena such as the sun, stars, and daybreak, as well as cultural "species": imagined ghosts, rainbow serpents, heroic ancestors; such eternal cultural verities as fires, spears, huts; and such human activities, conditions, or attributes as eating, vomiting, swimming, fighting, babies and corpses, milk and blood, lips and loins. While individual members of such totemic classes or species might disappear or be destroyed, the class itself was obviously ever-present and indestructible. The totems, therefore, lent permanence and stability to the clans, to the groupings of human individuals who generation after generation were each associated with a set of totems which distinguished one clan from another.

The stone axe was one of the most important of the many totems of the Sunlit Cloud Iguana clan. The names of many members of this clan referred to the axe itself, to activities in which the axe played a vital part, or to the clan's mythical ancestors with whom the axe was prominently associated. When it was necessary to represent the stone axe in totemic ceremonies, only men of this clan exhibited it or pantomimed its use. In secular life, the axe could be made by any man and used by all; but in the sacred realm of the totems it belonged exclusively to the Sunlit Cloud Iguana people.

3. The best, although highly concentrated, summaries of totemism among the Yir Yoront and the other tribes of north Queensland will be found in R. Lauriston Sharp, "Tribes and Totemism in Northeast Australia," *Oceania,* Vol. 8, 1939, pp. 254–275 and 439–461 (especially pp. 268–275); also "Notes on Northeast Australian Totemism," in *Papers of the Peabody Museum of American/Archaeology and Ethnology,* Vol. 20, *Studies in the Anthropology of Oceania and Asia,* Cambridge, 1943, pp. 66–71.

Supporting those aspects of cultural behavior which we have called technology and conduct, is a third area of culture which includes ideas, sentiments, and values. These are most difficult to deal with, for they are latent and covert, and even unconscious, and must be deduced from overt actions and language or other communicating behavior. In this aspect of the culture lies the significance of the stone axe to the Yir Yoront and to their cultural way of life.

The stone axe was an important symbol of masculinity among the Yir Yoront (just as pants or pipes are to us). By a complicated set of ideas the axe was defined as "belonging" to males, and everyone in the society (except untrained infants) accepted these ideas. Similarly spears, spear throwers, and fire-making sticks were owned only by men and were also symbols of masculinity. But the masculine values represented by the stone axe were constantly being impressed on all members of society by the fact that females borrowed axes but not other masculine artifacts. Thus the axe stood for an important theme of Yir Yoront culture: the superiority and rightful dominance of the male, and the greater value of his concerns and of all things associated with him. As the axe also had to be borrowed by the younger people it represented the prestige of age, another important theme running through Yir Yoront behavior.

To understand the Yir Yoront culture it is necessary to be aware of a system of ideas which may be called their totemic ideology. A fundamental belief of the aboriginal divided time into two great epochs: (1) a distant and sacred period at the beginning of the world when the earth was peopled by mildly marvelous ancestral beings or culture heroes who are in a special sense the forebears of the clans; and (2) a period when the old was succeeded by a new order which includes the present. Originally there was no anticipation of another era supplanting the present. The future would simply be an eternal continuation and reproduction of the present which itself had remained unchanged since the epochal revolution of ancestral times.

The important thing to note is that the aboriginal believed that the present world, as a natural and cultural environment, was and should be simply a detailed reproduction of the world of the ancestors. He believed that the entire universe "is now as it was in the beginning" when it was established and left by the ancestors. The ordinary cultural life of the ancestors became the daily life of the Yir Yoront camps, and the extraordinary life of the ancestors remained extant in the recurring symbolic pantomimes and paraphernalia found only in the most sacred atmosphere of the totemic rites.

Such beliefs, accordingly, opened the way for ideas of what *should be* (because it supposedly *was*) to influence or help determine what actually *is*. A man called Dog-chases-iguana-up-a-tree-and-barks-at-him-all-night had that and other names because he believed his ancestral alter ego had also had them; he was a member of the Sunlit Cloud Iguana clan because his ancestor was; he was associated with particular countries and totems of this same ancestor; during an initiation he played the role of a dog and symbolically attacked and killed certain members of other clans because his ancestor (conveniently either anthropomorphic or kynomorphic) really did the same to the ancestral alter egos of these men; and he would avoid his mother-in-law, joke with a mother's distant brother, and make spears in a certain way because his and other people's ancestors did these things. His behavior in these specific ways was outlined, and to that extent determined for him, by a set of ideas concerning the past and the relation of the present to the past.

But when we are informed that Dog-chases-etc. had two wives from the Spear Black Duck clan and one from the Native Companion clan, one of them being blind, that he had four children with such and such names, that he had a broken wrist and was left handed, all because his ancestor had exactly these same attributes, then we know (though he apparently didn't) that the present has influenced the past, that the mythical world has been somewhat adjusted to meet the exigencies and accidents of the inescapably real present.

There was thus in Yir Yoront ideology a nice balance in which the mythical was adjusted in part to the real world, the real world in part to the ideal pre-existing mythical world, the adjustments occurring to maintain a fundamental tenet of native faith that the present must be a mirror of the past. Thus the stone axe in all its aspects, uses, and associations was integrated into the context of Yir Yoront technology and conduct because a myth, a set of ideas, had put it there.

IV
THE OUTCOME

The introduction of the steel axe indiscriminately and in large numbers into the Yir Yoront technology occurred simultaneously with many other changes. It is therefore impossible to separate all the results of this single innovation. Nevertheless, a number of specific effects of the change from stone to steel axes may be noted, and the steel axe may be used as an epitome of the increasing quantity of European goods and implements received by the aboriginals and of their general influence on the native culture. The use of the steel axe to illustrate such influences would seem to be justified. It was one of the first Europe artifacts to be adopted for regular use by the Yir Yoront, and whether made of stone or steel, the axe was clearly one of the most important items of cultural equipment they possessed.

The shift from stone to steel axes provided no major technological difficulties. While the aboriginals themselves could not manufacture steel axe heads, a steady supply from outside continued; broken wooden handles could easily be replaced from bush timbers with aboriginal tools. Among the Yir Yoront the new axe was never used to the extent it was on mission or cattle stations (for carpentry work, pounding tent pegs, as a hammer, and so on); indeed, it had so few more uses than the stone axe that its practical effect on the native standard of living was negligible. It did some jobs better, and could be used longer without breakage. These factors were sufficient to make it of value to the native. The white man believed that a shift from steel to stone axe on his part would be a definite regression. He was convinced that his axe was much more efficient, that its use would save time, and that it therefore represented technical "progress" towards goals which he had set up for the native. But this assumption was hardly born out in aboriginal practice. Any leisure time the Yir Yoront might gain by using steel axes or other western tools was not invested in "improving the conditions of life," nor, certainly, in developing aesthetic activities, but in sleep—an art they had mastered thoroughly.

Previously, a man in need of an axe would acquire a stone axe head through regular trading partners from whom he knew what to expect, and was then dependent solely upon a known and adequate natural environment, and his own skills or easily acquired techniques. A man wanting a steel axe, however, was in no such self-reliant position. If he attended a mission festival when steel axes were handed out as gifts, he might receive one either by chance or by happening to impress upon the mission staff that he was one of the "better" bush aboriginals (the missionaries definition of "better" being quite different from that of his bush fellows). Or, again almost by pure chance, he might get some brief job in connection with the mission which would enable him to earn a steel axe. In either case, for older men a preference for the steel axe helped change the situation from one of self-reliance to one of dependence, and a shift in behavior from well-structured or defined situations in technology or conduct to ill-defined situations in conduct alone. Among the men, the older ones whose earlier experience or knowledge of the white man's harshness made them suspicious were particularly careful to avoid having relations with the mission, and thus excluded themselves from acquiring steel axes from that source.

In other aspects of conduct or social relations, the steel axe was even more significantly at the root of psychological stress among the Yir Yoront. This was the result of new factors which the missionary considered beneficial: the simple numerical increase in axes per capita as a result of mission distribution, and distribution directly to younger men, women, and even children. By winning the favor of the mission staff, a woman might be given a steel axe which was clearly intended to be hers, thus creating a situation quite different from the previous custom which necessitated her borrowing an axe from a male relative. As a result a woman would refer to the axe as "mine," a possessive form she was never able to use of the stone axe. In the same fashion, young men or even boys also obtained steel axes directly from the mission, with the result that older men no longer had a complete monopoly of all the axes in the bush community. All this led to a revolutionary confusion of sex, age, and kinship roles, with a major gain in independence and loss of subordination on the part of those who now owned steel axes when they had previously been unable to possess stone axes.

The trading partner relationship was also affected by the new situation. A Yir Yoront might have a trading partner in a tribe to the south whom he defined as a younger brother and over whom he would therefore have some authority. But if the partner were in contact with the mission or had other access to steel axes, his subordination obviously decreased. Among other things, this took some of the excitement away from the dry season fiesta-like tribal gatherings centering around initiations. These had traditionally been the climactic annual occasions for exchanges between trading partners, when a man might seek to acquire a whole year's supply of stone axe heads. Now he might find himself prostituting his wife to almost total strangers in return for steel axes or other white man's goods. With trading partnerships weakened, there was less reason to attend the ceremonies, and less fun for those who did.

Not only did an increase in steel axes and their distribution to women change the character of the relations between individuals (the paired relationships that have been noted), but a previously rare type of relationship was created in the Yir Yiront's conduct towards whites. In the aboriginal society there were few occasions outside of the immediate family when an individual would initiate action to several other people at once. In any average group, in accordance with the kinship system, while a person might be superordinate to several people to whom he could suggest or command action, he was also subordinate to several others with whom such behavior would be tabu. There was thus no overall chieftanship or authoritarian leadership of any kind. Such complicated operations as grass-burning animal drives or totemic ceremonies could be carried out smoothly because each person was aware of his role.

On both mission and cattle stations, however, the whites imposed their conception of leadership roles upon the aboriginals, consisting of one person in a controlling relationship with a subordinate group. Aboriginals called together to receive gifts, including axes, at a mission Christmas party found themselves facing one or two whites who sought to control their behavior for the occasion, who disregarded the age, sex, and kinship variables of which the aboriginals were so conscious, and who considered them all at one subordinate level. The white also sought to impose similar patterns on work parties. (However, if he placed an aboriginal in charge of a mixed group of post-hole diggers, for example, half of the group, those subordinate to the "boss," would work while the other half, who were superordinate to him, would sleep.) For the aboriginal, the steel axe and other European goods came to symbolize this new and uncomfortable form of social organization, the leader-group relationship.

The most disturbing effects of the steel axe, operating in conjunction with other elements also being introduced from the white man's several sub-cultures, developed in the realm of traditional ideas, sentiments and values. These were undermined at a rapidly mounting rate, with no new conceptions being defined to replace them. The result was the erection of a mental and moral void which foreshadowed the collapse and destruction of all Yir Yoront culture, if not, indeed, the extinction of the biological group itself.

From what has been said it should be clear how changes in overt behavior, in technology and conduct, weakened the values inherent in a reliance on nature, in the prestige of masculinity and of age, and in the various kinship relations. A scene was set in which a wife, or a young son whose initiation may not yet have been completed, need no longer defer to the husband or father who, in turn, became confused and insecure as he was forced to borrow a steel axe from them. For the woman and boy the steel axe helped establish a new degree of freedom which they accepted readily as an escape from the unconscious stress of the old patterns—but they too, were left confused and insecure. Ownership became less well defined with the result that stealing and trespassing were introduced into technology and conduct. Some of the excitement surrounding the great ceremonies evaporated and they lost their previous gaiety and interest. Indeed, life itself became less interesting, although this did not lead the Yir Yoront to discover suicide, a concept foreign to them.

The whole process may be most specifically illustrated in terms of totemic system, which also illustrates the significant role played by a system of ideas, in this case a totemic ideology in the breakdown of a culture.

In the first place, under pre-European aboriginal conditions where the native culture has become adjusted to a relatively stable environment, few, if any, unheard of or catastrophic crises can occur. It is clear, therefore, that the totemic system serves very effectively in inhibiting radical cultural changes. The closed system of totemic ideas, explaining, and categorizing a well-known universe as it was fixed at the beginning of time, presents a considerable obstacle to the adoption of new or the dropping of old culture traits. The obstacle is not insurmountable and the system allows for the minor variations which occur in the norms of daily life. But the inception of major changes cannot easily take place.

Among the bush Yir Yoront the only means of water transport is a light wood log to which they cling in their constant swimming of rivers, salt creeks, and tidal inlets. These natives know that tribes 45 miles further north have a bark canoe. They know these northern tribes can thus fish from midstream or out at sea, instead of clinging to the river banks and beaches, that they can cross coastal waters infested with crocodiles, sharks, sting rays, and Portuguese men-of-war without danger. They know the materials of which the canoe is made exist in their own environment. But they also know, as they say, that they do not have canoes because their own mythical ancestors did not have them. They assume that the canoe was part of the ancestral universe of the northern tribes. For them, then, the adoption of the canoe would not be simply a matter of learning a number of new behavioral skills for its manufacture and use. The adoption would require a much more difficult procedure; the acceptance by the entire society of a myth, either locally developed or borrowed, to explain the presence of the canoe, to associate it with some one or more of the several hundred mythical ancestors (and how decide which?), and thus establish it as an accepted totem of one of the clans ready to be used by the whole community. The Yir Yoront have not made this adjustment, and in this case we can only say that for the time being at least, ideas have won out over very real pressures for technological change. In the elaborateness and explicitness of the totemic ideologies we seem to have one explanation for the notorious stability of Australian cultures under aboriginal conditions, an explanation which gives due weight to the importance of ideas in determining human behavior.

At a later stage of the contact situation, as has been indicated, phenomena unaccounted for by the totemic ideological system begin to appear with regularity and frequency and remain within the range of native experience. Accordingly, they cannot be ignored (as the "Battle of the Mitchell" was apparently ignored), and there is an attempt to assimilate them and account for them along the lines of principles inherent in the ideology. The bush Yir Yoront of the mid-thirties represent this stage of the acculturation process. Still trying to maintain their aboriginal definition of the situation, they accept European artifacts and behavior patterns, but fit them into their totemic system, assigning them to various clans on a par with original totems. There is an attempt to have the myth-making process keep up with these cultural changes so that the idea system can continue to support the rest of the culture. But analysis of overt behavior, of dreams, and of some of the new myths indicates that this arrangement is not entirely satisfactory, that the native clings to his totemic system with intellectual loyalty (lacking any substitute ideology), but that associated sentiments and values are weakened. His attitudes towards his own and towards European culture are found to be highly ambivalent.

All ghosts are totems of the Head-to-the-East Corpse clan, are thought of as white, and are of course closely associated with death. The white man, too, is closely associated with death, and he and all things pertaining to him are naturally assigned to the Corpse clan as totems. The steel axe, as a totem, was thus associated with the Corpse clan. But as an "axe," clearly linked with the stone axe, it is a totem of the Sunlit Cloud Iguana clan. Moreover, the steel axe, like most European goods, has no distinctive origin myth, nor are mythical ancestors associated with it. Can anyone, sitting in the shade of a *ti* tree one afternoon, create a myth to resolve this confusion? No one has, and the horrid suspicion arises as to the authenticity of the origin myths, which failed to take into account this vast new universe of the white man. The steel axe, shifting hopelessly between one clan and the other, is not only replacing the stone axe physically, but is hacking at the supports of the entire cultural system.

The aboriginals to the south of the Yir Yoront have clearly passed beyond this stage. They are engulfed by European culture, either by the mission or cattle station sub-cultures or, for some natives, by a baffling, paradoxical combination of both incongruent varieties. The totemic ideology can no longer support the inrushing mass of foreign culture traits, and the myth-making process in its native form breaks down completely. Both intellectually and emotionally a saturation point is reached so that the myriad new traits which can neither be ignored nor any longer assimilated simply force the aboriginal to abandon his totemic system. With the collapse of this system of ideas, which is so closely related to so many other aspects of the native culture, there follows an appallingly sudden and complete cultural disintegration, and a demoralization of the individual such as has seldom been recorded elsewhere. Without the support of a system of ideas well devised to provide cultural stability in a stable environment, but admittedly too rigid for the new realities pressing in from outside, native behavior and native sentiments and values are simply dead. Apathy reigns. The aboriginal has passed beyond the realm of any outsider who might wish to do him well or ill.

Returning from the broken natives huddled on cattle stations or on the fringes of frontier towns to the ambivalent but still lively aboriginals settled on the Mitchell River mission, we note one further devious result of the introduction of European artifacts. During a wet season stay at the mission, the anthropologist discovered that his supply of tooth paste was being depleted at an alarming rate. Investigation showed that it was being taken by old men for use in a new tooth paste cult. Old materials of magic having failed, new materials were being tried out in a malevolent magic directed towards the mission staff and some of the younger aboriginal men. Old males, largely ignored by the missionaries, were seeking to regain some of their lost power and prestige. This mild aggression proved hardly effective, but perhaps only because confidence in any kind of magic on the mission was by this time at a low ebb.

For the Yir Yoront still in the bush, a time could be predicted when personal deprivation and frustration in a confused culture would produce an overload of anxiety. The mythical past of the totemic ancestors would disappear as a guarantee of a present of which the future was supposed to be a stable continuation. Without the past, the present could be meaningless and the future unstructured and uncertain. Insecurities would be inevitable. Reaction to this stress might be some form of symbolic aggression, or withdrawal and apathy, or some more realistic approach. In such a situation the missionary with understanding of the processes going on about him would find his opportunity to introduce his forms of religion and to help create a new cultural universe.

DISCUSSION QUESTIONS

1. What role did the stone axes play in traditional (precontact) Yir Yoront culture?
2. Which aspects of Yir Yoront society were altered (and in what ways) with the introduction of the steel axes?
3. Why is the concept of *integrated cultures* so important in today's world?

(http://infotrac.thomsonlearning.com/index.html)

You can find further relevant readings by searching *InfoTrac College Edition,* an online library with access to thousands of scholarly and popular periodicals. Below are suggested search terms for this article:

- Stone Age
- totemism

Anthropology Online: Wadsworth's Anthropology Resource Center

(http://anthropology.wadsworth.com)

The Wadsworth Anthropology Resource Center contains a wealth of information and useful tools for students including information on careers in anthropology.

15

The Price of Progress

JOHN BODLEY

For generations, governments of industrialized nations have financed foreign aid programs for less-affluent societies in Africa, Asia, and South America. While many of these programs over the years have been, at least in part, politically motivated, most have been predicated on the assumption that programs in areas of agricultural reform, public health, education, and family planning would lead to progress, modernization, and an increase in the quality of life. For the past several decades Professor John Bodley of Washington State University has challenged this fundamental assumption. By marshaling considerable anthropological data, Bodley documents how well-intentioned forces of change do not always have positive consequences. In this selection, Bodley demonstrates how certain development policies—which westerners uncritically see as forces for good in the world—can enrich some people at the expense of others. Bodley points out some of the more deleterious effects of development programs and policies on indigenous peoples, including disease of development, malnutrition, the degeneration of dental health, and ecological degradation.

This selection should not lead us to conclude that cultural anthropologists, in some naive attempt to preserve the pristine state of indigenous peoples, are against culture change. Rather it should serve as a reminder that many of us, particularly indigenous peoples, can become victims of progress. The answer is not to try to prevent change, but to ensure that those affected retain the right to choose their own lifestyles rather than having them imposed from the outside.

In aiming at progress . . . you must let no one suffer
by too drastic a measure, nor pay too high a price in upheaval
and devastation, for your innovation.

—MAUNIER, 1949:725

Until recently, government planners have always considered economic development and progress beneficial goals that all societies should want to strive toward. The social advantages of progress—as defined in terms of increased incomes, higher standards of living, greater security, and better health—are thought to be positive, *universal* goods, to be obtained at any price. Although one may argue that indigenous peoples must sacrifice their own cultures to obtain these benefits, government planners generally feel that this is a small price to pay for such obvious advantages.

In earlier chapters, evidence was presented to demonstrate that autonomous indigenous peoples have not *chosen* progress to enjoy its advantages, but that governments have *pushed* progress upon

From *Victims of Progress* by John Bodley, pp. 132–144. Used with permission.

them to obtain resources, not primarily to share the benefits of progress with indigenous peoples. It has also been shown that the price of forcing progress on unwilling recipients has involved the deaths of millions of indigenous people, as well as their loss of land, political sovereignty, and the right to follow their own lifestyle. This chapter does not attempt to further summarize that aspect of the cost of progress, but instead analyzes the specific effects of the participation of indigenous peoples in the worldmarket economy. In direct opposition to the usual interpretation, it is argued here that the benefits of progress are often both illusory and detrimental to indigenous peoples when they have not been allowed to control their own resources and define their relationship to the market economy.

PROGRESS AND THE QUALITY OF LIFE

One of the primary difficulties in assessing the benefits of progress and economic development for any culture is that of establishing a meaningful measure of both benefit and detriment. It is widely recognized that *standard of living,* which is the most frequently used measure of progress, is an intrinsically ethnocentric concept relying heavily upon indicators that lack universal cultural relevance. Such factors as GNP, per capita income, capital formation, employment rates, literacy, formal education, consumption of manufactured goods, number of doctors and hospital beds per thousand persons, and the amount of money spent on government welfare and health programs may be irrelevant measures of actual *quality* of life for autonomous or even semiautonomous small-scale cultures. In its 1954 report, the Trust Territory government indicated that since the Micronesian population was still largely satisfying its own needs within a cashless subsistence economy, "money income is not a significant measure of living standards, production, or well-being in this area" (TTR, 1953:44). Unfortunately, within a short time the government began to rely on an enumeration of specific imported consumer goods as indicators of a higher standard of living in the islands, even though many tradition-oriented islanders felt that these new goods symbolized a reduction of the quality of life.

A more useful measure of the benefits of progress might be based on a formula for evaluating cultures devised by Goldschmidt (1952:135). According to these less ethnocentric criteria, the important question to ask is: Does progress or economic development increase or decrease a given culture's ability to satisfy the physical and psychological needs of its population, or its stability? This question is a far more direct measure of quality of life than are the standard economic correlates of development, and it is universally relevant. Specific indication of this *standard* of living could be found for any society in the nutritional status and general physical and mental health of its population, the incidence of crime and delinquency, the demographic structure, family stability, and the society's relationship to its natural resource base. We might describe a society that has high rates of malnutrition and crime, and one that degrades its natural environment to the extent of threatening its continued existence, as having a lower standard of living than another society where these problems do not exist.

Careful examination of the data, which compare on these specific points the former condition of self-sufficient indigenous peoples with their condition following their incorporation into the world-market economy, leads to the conclusion that their standard of living is *lowered,* not raised, by economic progress—and often to a dramatic degree. This is perhaps the most outstanding and inescapable fact to emerge from the years of research that anthropologists have devoted to the study of culture change and modernization. Despite the best intentions of those who have promoted change and improvement, all too often the results have been poverty, longer working hours, and much greater physical exertion, poor health, social disorder, discontent, discrimination, overpopulation, and environmental deterioration—combined with the destruction of the small-scale culture. . . .

DISEASES OF DEVELOPMENT

> Perhaps it would be useful for public health specialists to start talking about a new category of diseases. . . . Such diseases could be called the "diseases of development" and would consist of those pathological conditions which are based on the usually unanticipated consequences of the implementation of developmental schemes.
>
> —HUGHES & HUNTER, 1972:93

Economic development increases the disease rate of affected peoples in at least three ways. First, to the extent that development is successful, it makes developed populations suddenly become vulnerable to all of the diseases suffered almost exclusively by "advanced" peoples. Among these are diabetes, obesity, hypertension, and a variety of circulatory problems. Second, development disturbs existing environmental balances and may dramatically increase some bacterial and parasite diseases. Finally, when development goals prove unattainable, an assortment of poverty diseases may appear in association with the crowded conditions of urban slums and the general breakdown in small-scale socioeconomic systems.

Outstanding examples of the first situation can be seen in the Pacific, where some of the most successfully transformed small-scale cultures are found. In Micronesia, where development has progressed more rapidly than perhaps anywhere else, between 1958 and 1972 the population doubled. However, the number of patients treated for heart disease in the local hospitals nearly tripled, mental disorder increased eightfold, and by 1972 hypertension and nutritional deficiencies began to make significant appearances for the first time (TTR, 1959, 1973, statistical tables).

Although some critics argue that the Micronesian figures simply represent better health monitoring due to economic progress, rigorously controlled data from Polynesia show a similar trend. The progressive acquisition of modern degenerative diseases was documented by an eight-member team of New Zealand medical specialists, anthropologists, and nutritionists, whose research was funded by the Medical Research Council of New Zealand and the World Health Organization. These researchers investigated the health status of a genetically related population at various points along a continuum of increasing cash income, modernizing diet, and urbanization. The extremes on this acculturation continuum were represented by the relatively traditional Pukapukans of the Cook Islands and the essentially Europeanized New Zealand Maori, and the busily developing Rarotongans, also of the Cook Islands, occupied the intermediate position. In 1971, after eight years of work, the team's preliminary findings were summarized by Dr. Ian Prior, cardiologist and leader of the research, as follows:

> We are beginning to observe that the more an islander takes on the ways of the West, the more prone he is to succumb to our degenerative diseases. In fact, it does not seem too much to say our evidence now shows that the farther the Pacific natives move from the quiet, carefree life of their ancestors, the closer they come to gout, diabetes, atherosclerosis, obesity, and hypertension.
>
> —PRIOR, 1971:2

In Pukapuka, where progress was limited by the island's small size and its isolated location some 480 kilometers from the nearest port, the annual per capita income was only about thirty-six dollars and the economy remained essentially at a subsistence level. Resources were limited and the area was visited by trading ships only three or four times a year; thus, there was little opportunity for intensive economic development. Predictably, the population of Pukapuka was characterized by relatively low levels of imported sugar and salt intake, and a presumably related low level of heart disease, high blood pressure, and diabetes. In Rarotonga, where economic success was introducing town life, imported food, and motorcycles, sugar and salt intakes nearly tripled, high blood pressure increased approximately ninefold, diabetes increased two- to threefold, and heart disease doubled for men and more than quadrupled for women. Meanwhile, the number of grossly obese women increased more than tenfold. Among the New Zealand Maori, sugar intake was nearly eight times that of the Pukapukans, gout in men was nearly double its rate on Pukapuka, diabetes in men was more than fivefold higher, and heart disease in women had increased more than sixfold. The Maori were, in fact, dying of "European" diseases at a greater rate than was the average New Zealand European.

Government development policies designed to bring about changes in local hydrology, vegetation, and settlement patterns and to increase population mobility, and even programs aimed at reducing some diseases, have frequently led to dramatic increases in disease rates because of the unforeseen effects of disturbing the preexisting order. Hughes and Hunter (1972) published an excellent survey of cases in which development led directly to increased disease rates in Africa. They concluded that hasty development intervention in relatively balanced local cultures and environments resulted in "a drastic deterioration in the social and economic conditions of life."

Self-sufficient populations in general have presumably learned to live with the endemic pathogens of their environments, and in some cases they have evolve genetic adaptations to specific diseases, such as the sickle-cell trait, which provided an immunity to malaria. Unfortunately, however, outside intervention has entirely changed this picture. In the late 1960s, the rate of incidence of sleeping sickness suddenly increased in many areas of Africa and even spread to areas where the disease had not formerly occurred, due to the building of new roads and migratory labor, both of which caused increased population movement. Forest-dwelling peoples such as the Aka in central Africa explicitly attribute new diseases such as AIDS and ebola to the materialism associated with roads and new settlements.

Large-scale relocation schemes, such as the Zande Scheme, had disastrous results when natives were moved from their traditional disease-free refuges into infected areas. Dams and irrigation developments inadvertently created ideal conditions for the rapid proliferation of snails carrying schistosomiasis (a liver fluke disease), and major epidemics suddenly occurred in areas where this disease had never before been a problem. DDT spraying programs have been temporarily successful in controlling malaria, but there is often a rebound effect that increases the problem when spraying is discontinued, and the malarial mosquitoes are continually evolving resistant strains.

Urbanization is one of the prime measures of development, but it is a mixed blessing for most small-scale cultures. Urban health standards are abysmally poor and generally worse than in rural areas for the former villagers who have crowded into the towns and cities throughout Africa, Asia, and Latin America seeking wage employment out of new economic necessity. Infectious diseases related to crowding and poor sanitation are rampant in urban centers, and greatly increased stress and poor nutrition aggravate a variety of other health problems. Malnutrition and other diet-related conditions are, in fact, one of the characteristic hazards of progress faced by indigenous peoples and are discussed in the following sections.

The Hazards of Dietary Change

The diets of indigenous peoples are admirably adapted to their nutritional needs and available food resources. Even though these diets may seem bizarre, absurd, and unpalatable to outsiders, they are unlikely to be improved by drastic modifications. Given the delicate balances and complexities involved in any subsistence system, change always involves risks, but for indigenous people the effects of dietary change have been catastrophic. . . .

Under normal conditions, food habits are remarkably resistant to change, and indeed people are unlikely to abandon their traditional diets voluntarily in favor of dependence on difficult-to-obtain exotic imports. In some cases it is true that imported foods may be identified with powerful outsiders and are therefore sought as symbols of greater prestige. This may lead to such absurdities as Amazonian Indians choosing to consume imported canned tuna fish when abundant high-quality fish is available in their own rivers. Another example of this situation occurs in tribes where mothers prefer to feed their infants expensive and nutritionally inadequate canned milk from unsanitary, but *high status,* baby bottles. The high status of these items is often promoted by clever traders and clever advertising campaigns.

Aside from these apparently voluntary changes, it appears that more often dietary changes are forced upon unwilling indigenous peoples by circumstances beyond their control. In some areas, new food crops have been introduced by government decree, or as a consequence of forced relocation or other policies designed to end hunting, pastoralism, or shifting cultivation. Food habits have also been modified by massive disruption of the natural environment by outsiders—as when sheepherders transformed the Australian Aborigines' foraging territory or when European invaders destroyed the bison herds that were the primary element in the Plains Indians' subsistence patterns. Perhaps the most frequent cause of diet change occurs when formerly self-sufficient peoples find that wage labor, cash cropping, and other economic development activities that feed resources into the world-market economy must inevitably divert time and energy away from the production of subsistence foods. Many indigenous peoples in transforming cultures suddenly discover that, like it or not, they are unable to secure traditional foods and must spend their newly acquired cash on costly and often nutritionally inferior manufactured foods.

Overall, the available data seem to indicate that the dietary changes that are linked to involvement in the world-market economy have tended to reduce rather than raise the nutritional levels of the affected peoples. Specifically, the vitamin, mineral, and protein components of their diets are often drastically reduced and replaced by enormous increases in starch and carbohydrates, often in the form of white flour and refined sugar.

Any deterioration in the quality of a given population's diet is almost certain to be reflected in an increase in deficiency diseases and a general decline in health status. Indeed, as indigenous peoples have shifted to a diet based on imported manufactured or processed foods, there has been a dramatic rise in malnutrition, a massive increase in dental problems, and a variety of other nutrition-related disorders. Nutritional physiology is so complex that even well-meaning dietary changes have had tragic consequences. In many areas of Southeast Asia, government-sponsored protein supplementation programs supplying milk to protein-deficient populations caused unexpected health problems and increased mortality. Officials failed to anticipate that in cultures where adults do not normally drink milk, the enzymes needed to digest it are no longer produced and milk *intolerance* results (Davis & Bolin, 1972). In Brazil, a similar milk distribution program caused an epidemic of permanent blindness by aggravating a preexisting vitamin A deficiency (Bunce, 1972).

Teeth and Progress

> There is nothing new in the observation that savages, or peoples living under primitive conditions, have, in general, excellent teeth. . . . Nor is it news that most civilized populations possess wretched teeth which begin to decay almost before they have erupted completely, and that dental caries is likely to be accompanied by periodontal disease with further reaching complications.
>
> —HOOTON, 1945:xviii

Anthropologists have long recognized that undisturbed indigenous peoples are often in excellent physical condition. And it has often been noted specifically that dental caries and the other dental abnormalities that plague global-scale societies are absent or rare among indigenous peoples who have retained their diets. The fact that indigenous food habits may contribute to the development of sound teeth, whereas modernized diets may do just the opposite, was illustrated as long ago as 1894 in an article in the *Journal of the Royal Anthropological Institute* that described the results of a comparison between the teeth of ten Sioux Indians and a comparable group of Londoners (Smith, 1894:109–116). The Indians were examined when they came to London as members of Buffalo Bill's Wild West Show and were found to be completely free of caries and in possession of all their teeth, even though half of the group were over thirty-nine years of age. Londoners' teeth were conspicuous for both their caries and their steady reduction in number with advancing age. The difference was attributed primarily to the wear and polishing caused by the Indian diet of coarse food and the fact that they chewed their food longer, encouraged by the absence of tableware.

One of the most remarkable studies of the dental conditions of indigenous peoples and the impact of dietary change was conducted in the 1930s by Weston Price (1945), an American dentist who was interested in determining what contributed to normal, healthy teeth. Between 1931 and 1936, Price systematically explored indigenous areas throughout the world to locate and examine the most isolated peoples who were still living relatively self-sufficiently. His fieldwork covered Alaska, the Canadian Yukon, Hudson Bay, Vancouver Island, Florida, the Andes, the Amazon, Samoa, Tahiti, New Zealand, Australia, New Caledonia, Fiji, the Torres Strait, East Africa, and the Nile. The study demonstrated both the superior quality of aboriginal dentition and the devastation that occurs as modern diets are adopted. In nearly every area where traditional foods were still being eaten, Price found perfect teeth with normal dental arches and virtually no decay, whereas caries and abnormalities increased steadily as new diets were adopted. In many cases the change was sudden and striking. Among Inuit (Eskimo) groups subsisting entirely on traditional food he found caries totally absent, whereas in groups eating a considerable quantity of store-bought food approximately 20 percent of their teeth were decayed. This figure rose to more than 30 percent with Inuit groups subsisting almost exclusively on purchased or government-supplied food and reached an incredible 48 percent among the native peoples of Vancouver Island. Unfortunately for many of these people, modern dental treatment did not accompany the new food, and their suffering was appalling. The loss of teeth was, of course, bad enough in itself, and it certainly undermined the population's resistance to many new diseases, including tuberculosis. But new foods were also accompanied by crowded, misplaced teeth, gum diseases, distortion of the face, and pinching of the nasal cavity. Abnormalities in the dental arch appeared in the new generation following the change in diet, while caries appeared almost immediately even in adults.

Price reported that in many areas the affected peoples were conscious of their own physical deterioration. At a mission school in Africa, the principal asked him to explain to the native schoolchildren why they were not physically as strong as children who had had no contact with schools. On an island in the Torres Strait the aborigines knew exactly what was causing their problems and resisted—almost to the point of bloodshed—government efforts to establish a store that would make imported food available. The government prevailed, however, and Price was able to establish a relationship between the length of time the government store had been established and the increasing incidence of caries among a population that had shown an almost 100 percent immunity to them before the store had been opened.

In New Zealand, the Maori, who in their aboriginal state are often considered to have been among the healthiest, most perfectly developed of peoples, were found to have "advanced" the furthest. According to Price:

> Their modernization was demonstrated not only by the high incidence of dental caries but also by the fact that 90 percent of the adults and 100 percent of the children had abnormalities of the dental arches.
>
> —PRICE, 1945:206

Malnutrition

Malnutrition, particularly in the form of protein deficiency, has become a critical problem for indigenous peoples who must adopt new economic patterns. Population pressures, cash cropping, and government programs all have tended to encourage the replacement of previous crops and other food sources that were rich in protein with substitutes high in calories but low in protein. In Africa, for example, protein-rich staples such as millet and sorghum are being replaced systematically by high-yielding manioc and plantains, which have insignificant amounts of protein. The problem is increased for cash croppers and wage laborers whose earnings are too low and unpredictable to allow purchase of adequate amounts of protein. In some rural areas, agricultural laborers have been forced systematically to deprive nonproductive members (principally children) of their households of minimal nutritional requirements to satisfy the need of the productive members of the household. This process has been documented in northeastern Brazil following the introduction of large-scale sisal plantations (Gross & Underwood, 1971). In urban centers, the difficulties of obtaining nutritionally adequate diets are even more serious for tribal immigrants, because costs are higher and poor quality foods often are more tempting.

One of the most tragic, and largely overlooked, aspects of chronic malnutrition is that it can lead to abnormally undersized brain development and apparently irreversible brain damage; chronic malnutrition has been associated with various forms of mental impairment or retardation. Malnutrition has been linked clinically with mental retardation in both Africa and Latin America (see, for example, Mönckeberg 1968), and this appears to be a worldwide phenomenon with serious implications (Montagu, 1972).

Optimistic supporters of progress will surely say that all of these new health problems are being overstressed and that the introduction of hospitals, clinics, and the other modern health institutions will overcome or at least compensate for all of these difficulties. However, it appears that uncontrolled population growth and economic impoverishment probably will keep most of these benefits out of reach for many indigenous peoples, and the intervention of modern medicine has at least partly contributed to the problem in the first place.

The generalization that global-scale culture frequently has a negative impact on the health of indigenous peoples has found broad empirical support worldwide (see especially Kroeger & Barbira-Freedman [1982] on Amazonia; Reinhard [1976] on the Arctic; and Wirsing [1985]), but these conclusions have not gone unchallenged. Some critics argue that the health of indigenous peoples was often poor before modernization, and they point specifically to low life expectancy and high infant mortality rates (see Edgerton, 1992). Demographic statistics on self-sufficient indigenous peoples are often problematic because precise data are scarce, but they do show a less favorable profile than that enjoyed by many global-scale societies. However, it should be remembered that our present life expectancy is a recent phenomenon that has been very costly in terms of medical research and technological advances. Furthermore, the benefits of our health system are not enjoyed equally by all members of our society. We could view the formerly high infant mortality rates as a relatively inexpensive and egalitarian small-scale public health program that offered the reasonable expectation of a healthy and productive life for those surviving to age fifteen.

Some critics also suggest that certain indigenous peoples, such as the New Guinea highlanders, were "stunted" by nutritional deficiencies created by their natural diet, which was "improved" through "acculturation" and cash cropping (Dennett & Connell, 1988). Although this argument suggests that the health question requires careful evaluation, it does not invalidate the empirical generalizations already established. Nutritional deficiencies undoubtedly occurred in densely populated zones in the central New Guinea highlands. However, the specific case cited above may not be widely representative of other indigenous groups even in New Guinea, and it does not address the facts of outside intrusion or the inequities inherent in the contemporary development process.

ECOCIDE

> "How is it," asked a herdsman . . . "how is it that these hills can no longer give pasture to my cattle? In my father's day they were green and cattle thrived there; today there is no grass and my cattle starve." As one looked one saw that what had once been a green hill had become a raw red rock.
>
> —JONES, 1934

Progress not only brings new threats to the health of indigenous peoples, it also imposes new strains on the ecosystems upon which they must depend for their ultimate survival. The introduction of new technology, increased consumption, reduced mortality rates, and the eradication of all previous controls have combined to replace what for many indigenous peoples was a relatively stable balance between population and natural resources, with a new system that is imbalanced. Economic development is forcing *ecocide* on peoples who were once careful stewards of their resources. There is already a trend toward widespread environmental deterioration in indigenous areas, involving resource depletion, erosion, plant and animal extinction, and a disturbing series of other previously unforeseen changes.

After the initial depopulation suffered by many indigenous peoples during their engulfment by frontiers of national expansion, their populations began to experience rapid growth. Authorities generally attribute this growth to the introduction of commercial medicine and new health measures and the termination of chronic intergroup violence, which reduced mortality rates, as well as to new technology, which increased food production. Certainly all of these factors played a part, but merely reducing mortality rates would not have produced the rapid population growth that most indigenous areas have experienced if traditional birth-spacing mechanisms had not been eliminated at the same time. Regardless of which factors were most important, it is clear that all of the natural and cultural checks on population growth have suddenly been pushed aside by culture change, while indigenous lands have been steadily reduced and consumption levels have risen. In many areas, environmental deterioration due to overuse of resources has set in, and in other areas such deterioration is imminent as resources continue to dwindle relative to the expanding population and increased use. Of course, population expansion by indigenous peoples may have positive political consequences, because where they can retain or regain their status as local majorities they may be in a more favorable position to defend their resources against intruders.

Swidden systems and pastoralism, both highly successful economic systems under former conditions, have proved particularly vulnerable to increased population pressures and outside efforts to raise productivity beyond its natural limits. Research in Amazonia demonstrates that population pressures and related resource depletion can be created indirectly by official policies that restrict the people of swidden systems to smaller territories. Resource depletion itself can then become a powerful means of forcing indigenous people into participating in the world-market economy—thus leading to further resource depletion. For example, Bodley and Benson (1979) showed how the Shipibo Indians in Peru were forced to further deplete their forest resources by cash cropping in the forest area to replace the resources that had been destroyed earlier by the intensive cash cropping necessitated by the narrow confines of their reserve. In this case, some species of palm trees that had provided critical housing materials were destroyed by forest clearing and had to be replaced by costly purchased materials. Research by Gross (1979) and others showed similar processes at work among four indigenous groups in central Brazil and demonstrated that the degree of market involvement increases directly with increases in resource depletion.

The settling of nomadic herders and the removal of prior controls on herd size have often led to serious overgrazing and erosion problems where these had not previously occurred. There are indications that the desertification problem in the Sahel region of Africa was aggravated by programs designed to settle nomads. The first sign of imbalance in a swidden system appears when the planting cycles are shortened to the point that garden plots are reused before sufficient forest regrowth can occur. If reclearing and planting continue in the same area, the natural patterns of forest succession may be disturbed irreversibly and the soil can be impaired permanently. An extensive tract of tropical rain forest in the lower Amazon of Brazil was reduced to a semiarid desert in just fifty years through such a process (Ackermann, 1964). The soils in the Azande area are also now seriously threatened with laterization and other problems as a result of the government-promoted cotton development scheme (McNeil, 1972).

The dangers of overdevelopment and the vulnerability of local resource systems have long been recognized by both anthropologists and indigenous peoples themselves, but the pressures for change have been overwhelming. In 1948, the Maya villagers of Chan Kom complained to Redfield (1962) about the shortening of their swidden cycles, which they correctly attributed to increasing population pressures. Redfield told them, however, that they had no choice but to go "forward with technology" (Redfield, 1962:178). In Assam, swidden cycles were shortened from an average of twelve years to only two or three within just twenty years, and anthropologists warned that the limits of swiddening would soon be reached (Burling, 1963:311–312). In the Pacific, anthropologists warned of population pressures on limited resources as early as the 1930s (Keesing, 1941:64–65). These warnings seemed fully justified, considering the fact that the crowded Tikopians were prompted by population pressures on their tiny island to suggest that infanticide be legalized. The warnings have been dramatically reinforced since then by the doubling of Micronesia's population in just the fourteen years between 1958 and 1972, from 70,600 to 114,645, while consumption levels have soared. By 1985, Micronesia's population had reached 162,321.

The environmental hazards of economic development and rapid population growth have become generally recognized only since worldwide concerns over environmental issues began in the early 1970s. Unfortunately, there is as yet little indication that the leaders of nations in transformation are sufficiently concerned with environmental limitations. On the contrary, governments are forcing indigenous peoples into a self-reinforcing spiral of population growth and intensified resource exploitation, which may be stopped only by environmental disaster or the total impoverishment of the indigenous peoples.

The reality of ecocide certainly focuses attention on the fundamental contrasts between small- and global-scale systems in their use of natural resources. In many respects the entire "victims of progress" issue hinges on natural resources, who controls them, and how they are managed. Indigenous peoples are victimized because they control resources that outsiders demand. The resources exist because indigenous people managed them conservatively. However, as with the issue of the health consequences of economic globalization, some anthropologists minimize the adaptive achievements of indigenous groups and seem unwilling to concede that ecocide might be a consequence of cultural change. Critics attack an exaggerated "noble savage" image of indigenous people living in perfect harmony with nature and having no visible impact groups do in fact modify the environment, and they conclude that there is no significant difference between how indigenous peoples and global-scale societies treat their environments. For example, Charles Wagley declared that Brazilian Indians such as the Tapirape

> are not "natural men." They have human vices just as we do. . . . They do not live "in tune" with nature any more than I do; in fact, they can often be as destructive of their environment, within their limitations, as some civilized men. The Tapirape are not innocent or childlike in any way.
>
> —WAGLEY, 1977:302

Anthropologist Terry Rambo demonstrated that the Semang of the Malaysian rain forests have a measurable impact on their environment. In his monograph *Primitive Polluters,* Rambo (1985) reported that the Semang live in smoke-filled houses. They sneeze and spread germs, breathe, and thus emit carbon dioxide. They clear small gardens, contributing "particulate matter" to the air and disturbing the local climate because cleared areas proved measurably warmer and drier than the shady forest. Rambo concluded that his research "demonstrates the essential functional similarity of the environmental interactions of primitive and civilized societies" (1985:78) in contrast to a "noble savage" view (Bodley, 1983) which, according to Rambo (1985:2), mistakenly "claims that traditional peoples almost always live in essential harmony with their environment."

This is surely a false issue. To stress, as I do, that small-scale cultures tend to manage their resources for sustained yield within relatively self-sufficient subsistence economies is not to portray them as either childlike or "natural." Nor is it to deny that small-scale cultures "disrupt" their environment and may never be in absolute "balance" with nature (Bodley, 1997c).

The ecocide issue is perhaps most dramatically illustrated by two sets of satellite photos taken over the Brazilian rain forests of Rondônia (Allard & McIntyre, 1988:780–781). Photos taken in 1973, when Rondônia was still a tribal domain, show virtually unbroken rain forest. The 1987 satellite photos, taken after just fifteen years of highway construction and "development" by outsiders, show more than 20 percent of the forest destroyed. The surviving Indians were being concentrated by FUNAI (Brazil's national Indian foundation) into what would soon become mere islands of forest in a ravaged landscape. It is irrelevant to quibble about whether indigenous peoples are noble, childlike, or innocent, or about the precise meaning of balance with nature, carrying capacity, or adaptation, to recognize that for the past 200 years rapid environmental deterioration on an unprecedented global scale has followed the wrestling of control of vast areas of the world from indigenous peoples by resource-hungry global-scale societies.

DEPRIVATION AND DISCRIMINATION

> Contact with European culture has given them a knowledge of great wealth, opportunity and privilege, but only very limited avenues by which to acquire these things.
>
> —CROCOMBE, 1968

Unwittingly, indigenous peoples have had the burden of perpetual relative deprivation thrust upon them by acceptance—either by themselves or by the governments administering them—of the standards of socioeconomic progress set for them by the global-scale cultures. By comparison with the material wealth of commercial societies, small-scale societies become, by definition, impoverished. They are then forced to transform their cultures and work to achieve what many economists now acknowledge to be unattainable goals. Even though in many cases the modest GNP goals set by economic planners for the impoverished nations during the "development decade" of the 1960s were often met, the results were hardly noticeable for most of the indigenous people involved. Population growth, environmental limitations, inequitable distribution of wealth, and the continued rapid growth of the global-scale cultures have all meant that both the absolute and the relative gap between the rich and poor in the world is steadily widening. The prospect that indigenous peoples will actually be able to attain the levels of resource consumption to which they are being encouraged to aspire is remote indeed except for those few groups that have retained effective control over strategic mineral resources.

Indigenous peoples may feel deprivation not only when the economic goals they have been encouraged to seek fail to materialize, but also when they discover that they are powerless, second-class citizens who are discriminated against and exploited by the dominant society. At the same time, they are denied the satisfactions of their small-scale cultures, because these have been sacrificed in the process of globalization. Under the impact of major economic change, family life is disrupted, previous social controls are often lost, and many indicators of social anomie such as alcoholism, crime, delinquency, suicide, emotional disorders, and despair may increase. The inevitable frustration resulting from this continual deprivation finds expression in the cargo cults, revitalization movements, and a variety of other political and religious movements that have been widespread among indigenous peoples following their disruption by the economic globalization process.

DISCUSSION QUESTIONS

1. What criteria does Bodley use to measure progress? How do they differ from the criteria typically used by governments to measure progress?
2. What are some of the harmful effects of dietary change on local populations?
3. What does Bodley mean by the term *ecocide?* Give some examples.

RESOURCES ON THE INTERNET

InfoTrac College Edition

(http://infotrac.thomsonlearning.com/index.html)

You can find further relevant readings by searching *InfoTrac College Edition,* an online library with access to thousands of scholarly and popular periodicals. Below are suggested search terms for this article:

- standard of living
- dietary change
- ecocide

Anthropology Online: Wadsworth's Anthropology Resource Center

(http://anthropology.wadsworth.com)

The Wadsworth Anthropology Resource Center contains a wealth of information and useful tools for students including information on careers in anthropology.